TOP MARKS

11 +

MATHS

PRACTICE MAKES

PERFECT

WORKBOOK WITH OVER 500 QUESTIONS ON TOPICS FREQUENTLY TESTED IN THE 11+

(WITH ANSWERS)

By Jane Stone

ISBN : 9781672683838

Contents

Introduction

Why choose this book?

I am a qualified teacher, with over eighteen year's teaching experience, who has been tutoring children for the 11+ exam for over 11 years. During this time, I have gained a very good understanding regarding the support they need in order to thoroughly prepare for the exam.

Following the publication of my verbal reasoning book, I turned my attention to maths. Once again, I found that more practice questions were needed to help children master the skills required to pass the 11+. Many of the topics required for the test are new to the children. Therefore, they need clear explanations and repetition to aid their learning.

My students have benefited from this approach and gain confidence and understanding as they work through the questions. The vast majority pass the paper each year, with some achieving scores exceeding 90%.

My overall pass rate in the 11+ is very high so feel I must be doing something right!

My new book contains over 500 questions covering a wide range of the topics tested. I hope that it can guide your child to success. Always remember…..

Practice Makes Perfect!

Good luck.

1. Calculating Fractions of a Whole Number

To find a fraction of an amount divide the total amount by the denominator (bottom number) and then multiply the answer by the numerator (top number).

Eg: 3/8 of 40 = 40 ÷ 8 = 5 x 3 = 15

Always read the question carefully.

Are you finding the fraction stated in the question? Or, is it a multi-step problem so you are using this answer to calculate the final answer?

Eg: There are 120 children in a school year group. 3/5 go on a school trip. How many children is this?

This question is asking how many **go** on the trip so find 3/5 of 120.

120 ÷ 5 = 24 x 3 = 72

Answer : 72

HOWEVER.....if the question said:

120 children are in a school year group. 3/5 go on a school trip how many stay at school?

The calculation would be different. In this question you are finding those who **stay** at school.

To solve the problem you can either work out the fraction who stay ie

1 – 3/5 = 2/5

Then calculate 2/5 of 120 :

120 ÷ 5 = 24 x 2 = 48

OR find the 3/5 who go and subtract from 120.

120 ÷ 5 = 24 x 3 = 72

120 – 72 = 48

Answer : 48

1. In a shoe shop 124 pairs of shoes were sold on Saturday of which ¼ were size 5. How many size 5 shoes were sold?

    A. 28   B. 30   C. 31   D. 60   E. 62

2. In a class of 32 children 5/8 hand their homework in on time. How many do not hand theirs in on time?

    A. 12   B. 16   C. 18   D. 20   E. 22

3. A sandwich bar sells 380 sandwiches one lunchtime of which 1/5 are cheese and tomato, 3/10 are chicken salad and the rest are egg and cress. How many egg and cress sandwiches did they sell?

    A. 38   B. 76   C. 114   D. 190   E. 234

4. In a year of 161 children 5/7 belong to a school club. How many do not belong to a club?

    A. 23   B. 46   C. 69   D. 92   E. 115

5. Of the 4500 people at a football match 6/9 buy a hot drink at half time. How many people is this?

    A. 1500   B. 1750   C. 2000   D. 2500   E. 3000

6. In a cinema there are 427 seats of which 2/7 are empty. How many people are in the cinema?

    A. 61   B. 122   C. 208   D. 305   E. 366

7. In the month of April, it snowed for 1/6 of the days. How many days did it snow for?

    A. 4   B. 5   C. 6   D. 8   E. 10

8. A baker bakes 135 loaves. 2/5 are wholegrain, 1/3 are seeded and the rest are white loaves. How many white loaves did he bake?

    A. 36   B. 37   C. 45   D. 54   E. 99

9. Sarah receives £96 for her birthday. She saves 3/8 of it and spends the rest. How much does she spend?

   A.   £36   B.   £48   C.   £56   D.   £60   E.   £72

10. 200 children take part in sports day. ¼ take part in a running race, 5/8 take part in a field event. The rest take part in fun events. How many take part in a field event?

    A.   25   B.   50   C.   100   D.   125   E.   150

11. 200 children take part in sports day. ¼ take part in a running race, 5/8 take part in a field event. The rest take part in fun events. How many take part in the fun events?

    A.   25   B.   50   C.   100   D.   125   E.   150

12. A jigsaw puzzle has 789 pieces. Claire has completed 2/3 of the puzzle. How many pieces remain in the box?

    A.   245   B.   263   C.   342   D.   375   E.   423

13. A teacher marks 40 pieces of English work. 1/5 are essays, 1/8 are poems, 1/10 are stories and the rest are reports. How many reports does she mark?

    A.   4   B.   5   C.   8   D.   13   E.   23

14. In September it was sunny for 8/15 of the days. How many sunny days were there?

    A.   14   B.   15   C.   16   D.   17   E.   18

15. A book contains 550 pages. 3/11 of the pages have illustrations. How many pages is this?

    A.   50   B.   100   C.   150   D.   200   E.   350

16. A hotel has 456 rooms. 2/3 are full. How any empty rooms are there?

    A.   75   B.   126   C.   152   D.   194   E.   304

17. A farmer has 80 acres of land. ¼ of the land is used to grow wheat, 3/5 to grow barley and the rest is used to grow corn. How many acres are used to grow corn?

    A.   12   B.   18   C.   20   D.   36   E.   48

18. In a class of 28 children 4/7 are right-handed. How many are left-handed?

    A.   10   B.   12   C.   14   D.   16   E. 18

19. A supermarket has 2412 customers in one day. Of these 4/6 pay by credit card, the rest pay by cash. How many people pay with cash?

    A.   402   B.   804   C.   1206   D.   1402   E. 1804

20. A zoo has 770 animals. 7/10 are mammals, 1/5 are reptiles and the rest are birds. How many birds are there in the zoo?

    A.   77   B.   154   C.   208   D.   462   E. 539

21. 4/9 of a variety bag of crisps are salt and vinegar flavour. If there are 27 packets in the bag how many packets are of a different flavour?

    A.   12   B.   13   C.   14   D.   15   E. 16

22. A florist sells 147 bouquets on Mother's Day. 5/7 of them contain carnations. How many bouquets do not contain carnations?

    A.   21   B.   42   C.   75   D.   105   E. 120

23. In a week Carl spends 1/3 of his time sleeping. How many hours does he sleep for?

    A.   24   B.   48   C.   56   D.   72   E. 96

24. Rita owns 48 pairs of shoes. 1/6 are white, 3/12 are brown, 3/8 are black the remainder are blue. How many pairs of blue shoes does she have?

    A.   8   B.   10   C.   12   D.   16   E. 18

25. Jodie has 5/9 of £180. Faith has 6/7 of £210. How much more does Faith have than Jodie?

    A.   £50   B.   £65   C.   £75   D.   £80   E. £85

26. Each month Mark gets £20 pocket money and earns £50. He spends 3/7 of his money on books and 1/5 on CDs. He saves the rest. How much money does he save?

    A.   £14   B.   £26   C.   £30   D.   £34   E. £45

27. A swimming pool has a capacity of 350 000 litres of water. The pool has a leak and loses 2/7 of the water. How much water, in litres, is left in the pool?

   A. 50 000   B. 100 000   C. 150 000   D. 200 000   E. 250 000

28. In a test Mia answers 8/9 of the questions. If there are 45 questions, how many does she answer?

   A.   5   B.   24   C.   36   D.   40   E. 42

29. In a forest of 900 trees, 1/6 are evergreen, the rest are deciduous. How many trees are deciduous?

   A.   100   B.   150   C.   300   D.   500   E. 750

30. In a baker's window there are 104 items. 3/8 of them are cakes, ¼ are biscuits and the rest are loaves of bread. How many loaves are there?

   A.   13   B.   26   C.   39   D.   52   E. 65

2. Simplifying Fractions

Example :

In a theatre there are 480 seats. 360 are booked for the evening performance. Give this fraction in its lowest terms.

Solution :

Write the fraction as it is stated in the question:

360 / 480

Now simplify this. What number can divide into both numerator and denominator?

Both are multiples of 10 so 360 ÷ 10 = 36

$$480 ÷ 10 = 48$$

36/48 can be further simplified as 12 is a factor of both numbers.

36 ÷ 12 = 3

48 ÷ 12 = 4

Answer: 3/4

You may recognise that 120 will divide into both numerator and denominator.

So 360 ÷ 120 = 3

480 ÷ 120 = 4

Remember......
Lowest terms and simplest form mean the same thing.

1. In a doctor's waiting room there are 45 patients of which 25 are male. What fraction of the patients are male? Give this as a fraction in its lowest terms.

   A.   1/3   B.   3/4   C.   5/9   D.   4/7   E. 4/9

2. A florist makes 150 bouquets a week. 60 of these contain roses. What fraction of the bouquets contain roses? Give your answer as a fraction in its simplest form.

   A.   1/5   B.   2/5   C.   3/5   D.   2/10   E. 8/10

3. In a test of 85 questions Simon answered 70 questions correctly. What fraction did he get incorrect? Give your answer in its lowest terms.

   A.   14/17   B.   8/20   C.   6/25   D.   3/17   E. 4/25

4. A factory makes 3300 light bulbs a day. 30 are damaged and cannot be sold. What fraction cannot be sold? Give the answer in its simplest form.

   A.   3/110   B.   1/90   C.   3/90   D.   2/110   E. 1/110

5. A strawberry grower picks 50kg of strawberries a day of which 2kg are not ripe enough to sell. What fraction does he sell? Give the answer in its lowest terms.

   A.   24/25   B.   1/25   C.   24/50   D.   23/25   E. 20/25

6. A theatre can hold 420 people, 120 seats are empty. What fraction is this in its simplest form?

   A.   1/6   B.   2/7   C.   5/7   D.   6/7   E.   5/6

7. 300 hot air balloons take part in a festival of these 180 are red in colour. What fraction are not red? Give your answer in its lowest terms.

   A.   2/5   B.   3/10   C.   3/18   D.   3/5   E.   4/18

8. In a box of 32 chocolates, 14 are milk chocolate. What fraction is this in its simplest form?

   A.   14/30   B.   3/14   C.   7/16   D.   9/16   E.   2/3

9. A nursery grows 15000 plants a year of which 1200 are killed by frost. What fraction survive? Give the answer in its lowest terms.

   A.   3/4   B.   23/25   C.   5/6   D.   7/15   E.   2/25

10. In a restaurant there are 84 tables. 70 tables are booked one evening. What fraction is this in its simplest form?

   A.   1/6   B.   7/8   C.   8/9   D.   5/6   E.   7/9

11. In a chess club of 45 members 39 are male. Give this as a fraction in its lowest terms.

   A.   13/14   B.   5/8   C.   7/15   D.   13/15   E.   7/8

12. 95 questionnaires were sent out. Of these, 60 were completed and returned. Write this as a fraction in its simplest form.

   A.   7/9   B.   12/19   C.   6/9   D.   3/8   E. 5/9

13. In a year group of 180 children, 24 do not have pets. What fraction of the year group do have pets? Give your answer in its lowest terms.

   A.   11/18   B.   13/18   C.   13/15   D.   14/15   E. 2/15

14. In a theatre there are 240 seats. The evening performance has 32 empty seats. How many seats are occupied? Write this as a fraction in its simplest form.

   A.   13/15   B.   8/15   C.   2/15   D.   4/24   E. 7/10

15. In a test Ellie scores 27/36. Write this as fraction in its lowest terms.

   A.   5/9   B.   7/8   C.   5/6   D.   3/4   E. 6/7

16. Before lunch, a postman delivers 150 of the 210 letters in his sack. What fraction remains to be delivered? Give you answer in its simplest form.

   A.   1/7   B.   2/7   C.   5/7   D.   1/3   E. 2/3

17. In a survey of 108 people 45 said their favourite colour was red. Write this as a fraction in its lowest terms.

   A.   17/36   B.   11/12   C.   5/12   D.   19/36   E. 7/12

18. At a car-boot sale Bill sells 63 of his 140 items. What fraction is unsold? Give your answer in its simplest form.

   A.   9/20   B.   11/20   C.   7/20   D.   11/14   E. 9/14

19. 400 raffle tickets were sold at a school fair. Of these, 80 win a prize. What fraction is this in its lowest terms?

   A.   1/7   B.   1/3   C.   1/9   D.   1/5   E. 1/8

20. In a restaurant there are 48 tables. 42 of them are booked for lunch. Write this as a fraction in its simplest form.

   A.   5/12   B.   7/12   C.   3/8   D.   5/8   E. 7/8

21. In the month of September there were 22 sunny days. Write this as a fraction in its lowest terms.

   A.   7/15   B.   11/15   C.   22/31   D.   13/15   E. 9/31

22. In a sweet shop 55 out of the 121 sweets sold were chocolates. What is this as a fraction in its simplest form?

   A.   11/12   B.   5/12   C.   7/11   D.   3/12   E. 5/11

23. In a gymnastics competition 8 out of the 60 competitors withdrew due to illness. What fraction competed in the competition. Give this fraction in its lowest terms.

   A.   13/15   B.   7/15   C.   4/6   D.   2/15   E. 5/6

24. A shoe shop sold 87 pairs of shoes on Saturday. Of these 42 pairs were size 5. What fraction sold were size 5? Give your answer in its simplest form.

   A.   42/129   B.   15/29   C.   14/29   D.   14/129   E. 3/4

25. A doctor sees 32 patients in a morning. 20 require a prescription. What fraction do not need medicine? Give the fraction in its lowest terms.

   A.   2/8   B.   1/8   C.   5/8   D.   3/8   E. 7/8

26. Mum spent £95 on shopping last week. She spent £50 in the supermarket and the rest in other shops. What fraction of the total amount did she spend in other shops? Give the fraction in its simplest form.

   A.   9/19   B.   10/19   C.   50/95   D.   11/15   E. 9/15

27. A netball team wins 18 matches, drew 10 and lost 4. What fraction of its matches did it draw? Give the fraction its lowest terms.

   A.   3/8   B.   9/16   C.   3/16   D.   1/8   E. 5/16

28. The following year, the same netball team won 20 matches, drew 9 and lost 7. What fraction did it draw this year? Give your answer in its lowest terms.

    A.   1/3   B.   1/4   C.   1/5   D.   3/4   E. 2/5

29. Mrs Smith plants 72 seeds. 56 grow, the rest fail to germinate. What fraction of the seeds do not grow?

    A.   7/9   B.   2/7   C.   2/9   D.   3/7   E. 3/5

30. Carla buys 38 party bags for a birthday party. 32 children come to the party. What fraction of the bags does she give out? Give the fraction in its lowest terms.

    A.   15/16   B.   11/16   C.   12/19   D.   16/19   E. 3/19

3. Converting Fractions into Percentages

Remember that percent means out of one hundred. Convert the fraction into its equivalent fraction, in hundredths, then multiply by 100 to find the percentage.

Example 1

18 children in a class of 30 own a pet. What percentage is this?

Solution : 18/30 = 6/10 = 60/100 = 60%

Answer : 60%

Example 2

A gym has 250 members. 120 are male. What percentage of the members are female?

Solution : Find the number of female members. Write as a fraction. Simplify. multiply by 100.

250 – 120 = 130.

130/250 = 26/50 = 52/100 = 52%

Answer : 52%

Example 3

5 out of 8 people voted in an election. What percentage is this?

Solution : Write as a fraction. Convert to a decimal. Multiply by 100.

5/8 = 0.625 = 62.5%

Answer : 62.5%

1. Charlotte scores 17/25 in a test. What percentage is this?

    A.   60%   B.   64%   C.   68%   D.   72%   E. 76%

2. A social club has 60 members, of which, 42 are female. What percentage are male?

    A.   20%   B.   30%   C.   40%   D.   60%   E. 70%

3. If a fast food delivery service has delivered 45 out of 50 meals, what percentage remain to be delivered?

    A.   10%   B.   35%   C.   60%   D.   80%   E. 90%

4. A secretary has typed 21 out of the 30 letters in her in-tray. What percentage is this?

    A.   60%   B.   64%   C.   68%   D.   70%   E. 74%

5. A baker bakes 200 loaves in a morning. Of these, 170 have sold by lunchtime. What percentage are unsold?

    A.   10%   B.   15%   C.   60%   D.   85%   E. 90%

6. A container is 20% full and holds 5 litres of water. How much water, in litres, will the container hold when it is completely full?

    A.   10   B.   15   C.   20   D.   25   E. 30

7. A petrol tank is 30% full and contains 12 gallons of fuel. How much fuel can the tank hold when it is completely full?

    A.   24   B.   36   C.   40   D.   45   E.   48

8. A cake is divided into 12 slices. I eat 2 slices and my friend eats 1 slice. What percentage of the cake has been eaten?

    A.   10%   B.   15%   C.   20%   D.   25%   E.   75%

9. A book has 450 pages. I have read 135 pages. What percentage remains to be read?

    A.   30%   B.   40%   C.   55%   D.   60%   E.   70%

10. A cinema holds 250 people and 185 seats are taken. What percentage is this?

    A.   74%   B.   64%   C.   54%   D.   94%   E.   84%

11. 18 out of the 30 children in a class have brothers or sisters. What percentage do not have a brother or sister?

    A.   36%   B.   40%   C.   48%   D.   54%   E.   60%

12. Sarah scores 17/20 in a test. What percentage does she get?

    A.   79%   B.   82%   C.   85%   D.   87%   E. 89%

13. Claire completes 4 pieces of homework, in one evening. If she has 10 pieces of homework a week, what percentage must she still complete?

    A.   35%   B.   40%   C.   45%   D.   60%   E. 65%

14. The local amateur dramatics club has 80 members. Of these, 56 members are women. What percentage is this?

    A.   60%   B.   65%   C.   70%   D.   75%   E. 80%

15. A school hall can hold 500 children. 450 children are in the hall. What percentage is this?

    A.   55%   B.   65%   C.   70%   D.   75%   E. 90%

16. Mrs. Brown is making cakes for a school fete. She has made 70 cakes and decorated 49 of them. What percentage remains to be decorated?

    A.   15%   B.   20%   C.   30%   D.   60%   E. 70%

17. Ben shares a packet of sweets with his friends. There are 30 sweets in the bag and Ben eats 9 of them. What percentage are eaten by his friends?

    A.   30%   B.   40%   C.   55%   D.   60%   E. 70%

18. Zoe runs a dance school. Of the 55 students, 44 attend lessons once a week. What percentage is this?

    A.   20%   B.   40%   C.   60%   D.   80%   E. 90%

19. The local library has 12,000 books. 9,000 are fiction, the remainder are non-fiction. What percentage of the books are non-fiction?

    A.   20%   B.   25%   C.   45%   D.   75%   E. 80%

20. A driving instructor has 15 students taking a driving test. Of these, 12 pass. What percentage do not pass the test?

   A.   18%   B.   20%   C.   35%   D.   70%   E.   80%

21. In a town, with a population of 30 000, 900 residents are not members of the residents' association. What percentage is this?

   A.   3%   B.   2%   C.   1%   D.   8%   E.   5%

22. An artist sells 27 of the 30 paintings he exhibits. What percentage are not sold?

   A.   10%   B.   40%   C.   60%   D.   70%   E.   90

23. In a week, there are 2000 visitors to a museum. 80 pay a reduced entrance fee. What percentage is this?

   A.   2%   B.   4%   C.   8%   D.   12%   E.   20%

24. A school has 800 pupils. 8 leave during the autumn term. What percentage is this?

   A.   0.5%   B.   1%   C.   1.5%   D.   2%   E.   3%

25. 24 out of 200 people surveyed chose fruit as their favourite snack. What percentage chose fruit?
   A.   8%   B.   10%   C.   12%   D.   14%   E.   16%

26. 300 ice creams are sold in a day. 60 of them are vanilla. What percentage are not vanilla?

   A.   15%   B.   20%   C.   40%   D.   65%   E.   80%

27. 60 animals visit a vet. 15 of these are rabbits. What percentage are rabbits?
   A.   15%   B.   20%   C.   25%   D.   30%   E.   40%

28. 400 books are borrowed from the local library. 56 of them are children's books. What percentage is this?

   A.   14%   B.   12%   C.   11%   D.   16%   E.   18%

29. In a test Martin scores 21 out of 25. What percentage of the questions did he get incorrect?

    A.   8%   B.   16%   C.   32%   D.   66%   E. 84%

30. A sports stadium is 60% full and has 120 000 people in it. How many people will it hold when full?

A.	140 000	B.	160 000	C.	180 000
D.	200 000	E.	240 000			

4. Finding Percentages of Amounts

Example 1

Alice receives 3% interest per year on her savings. If she has £1500 in the bank, how much interest will she receive this year?

Solution: Divide £1500 by 100 to find 1%. Multiply the answer by 3 to find 3%.

£1500 ÷ 100 = £15

£15 x 3 = £45

Answer: £45

Example 2

In a sale a coat is reduced by 15%. Before the sale the coat cost £120. What would the cost be in the sale?

Solution A : Find 10 %. Halve to find 5%. Add together. Subtract from £120.

£120 ÷ 10 = £12 (10%)

£12 ÷ 2 = £6 (5%)

15% = £18

£120 - £18 = £102

Answer : £102

Solution B : Divide £120 by 100 to find 1%. Multiply by 15 to get 15%. Subtract from £120.

£120 ÷ 100 = £1.20

£1.20 x 15 = £18

£120 - £18 = £102

1. Susan plants 60 runner bean plants. 35% are eaten by slugs. How many plants survive?

    A.   18   B.   21   C.   27   D.   36   E. 39

2. 15% of a box of chocolates have been eaten. If the box contains 40 chocolates when full, how many have been eaten?

   A.   6   B.   4   C.   10   D.   15   E. 12

3. In a sale, 20% is deducted from the price of a television. If the television was £350 before the sale, how much would it be now?

   A.   £60   B.   £70   C.   £180   D.   £280   E. £305

4. Of the 400 visitors to a zoo one day, 85% are children. How many children visited the zoo?

   A.   190   B.   240   C.   270   D.   310   E. 340

5. 75% of the 56 tables in a restaurant are booked one evening. How many empty tables are there?

   A.   10   B.   14   C.   24   D.   42   E. 44

6. A factory produces 3400 light bulbs every hour. 5% of these are broken and unable to be sold. How many light bulbs can be sold?

   A.   3230   B.   2340   C.   1170   D.   340   E. 170

7. Mary earns £120 in one day and saves 60% of it. How much money does she save?

   A.   £48   B.   £56   C.   £69   D.   £72   E. £84

8. In a school year group there are 168 children, of which, 75% have school lunch and the remainder bring their own. How many children bring their own lunch?

   A.   32   B.   42   C.   60   D.   86   E. 126

9. A local business decides to donate some of its profits to charity. In a year, they make £45,000 profit and give 3% to a local charity. How much money do they donate?

   A.   £900   B.   £1150   C.   £1350   D.   £1800   E. £2250

10. A theatre holds 620 people when full. 85% of the seats arc booked for a performance. How many seats have been booked?

   A.   486   B.   496   C.   502   D.   527   E. 536

11. Mandy surveys 80 people about their favourite colour. 5% say their favourite colour is orange. How many people chose a different colour?

    A.   4   B.   8   C.   40   D.   64   E. 76

12. A beauty salon has 50 appointments booked in one day. 4% are cancelled. How many cancellations are there?

    A.   1   B.   2   C.   3   D.   4   E. 5

13. Jack has read 30% of his book. If the book contains 760 pages, how many pages remain to be read?

    A.   218   B.   228   C.   376   D.   418   E. 532

14. A garden centre sells 280 trays of plants. 45% are primroses. How many trays of primroses are sold?

    A.   126   B.   112   C.   135   D   142   E. 140

15. 70% of the 50 passengers on a coach journey are travelling alone. How many people are not travelling alone?

    A.   10   B.   15   C.   30   D.   35   E. 40

16. In the month of November it rained for 40% of the days. How many days did it not rain for?

    A.   12   B.   14   C.   16   D.   18   E. 20

17. A bookcase holds 550 books. If it is 80% full, how many more books can be put on the bookcase?

    A.   55   B.   110   C.   220   D.   330   E. 440

18. 24,000 people attend a football match. Of these 64% are season ticket holders. How many people at the match have a season ticket?

    A.   14 400   B.   14 880   C.   15 360
    D.   15 840   E.   16 220

19. A local radio station plays 300 records in a day. If 35% are classical music and the remainder are pop music, how many pop records does it play?

    A.   30   B.   45   C.   90   D.   145   E. 195

20. In a class of 40 children 85% hand their homework in on time. How many children hand their homework in late?

  A. 6   B. 4   C. 8   D. 34   E. 36

21. A dentist sees 25 patients in a day. 20% do not need treatment. How many people do require treatment?

  A. 5   B. 10   C. 18   D. 20   E. 22

22. A golfer loses 7% of his golf balls in a year. He starts the year with 200 balls. How many does he have at the end of the year?

  A. 186   B. 180   C. 140   D. 114   E. 188

23. Terry has 40 stickers in his collection. He gives 15% to his brother and 10% to his sister. How many does he now have?

  A. 4   B. 6   C. 10   D. 20   E. 30

24. 8% of the pages in a book contain illustrations. The book has 750 pages. How many pages have illustrations?

  A. 45   B. 60   C. 65   D. 75   E. 90

25. 28 300 people vote in an election. 2% do not complete the form correctly and have their votes disallowed. How many votes were allowed?

  A. 27 407   B. 27 648   C. 27 734
  D. 27 910   E. 28 102

26. In a survey, 23% of people said their favourite fruit was a strawberry. If 500 people were Surveyed, how many people preferred strawberries?

  A. 100   B. 115   C. 365   D. 385   E. 405

27. 89% of 40 000 people have a bank account. How many people do not have a bank account?

  A. 4000   B. 4200   C. 4400   D. 4600   E. 4800

28. In a quiz, a contestant answers 74% of the questions correctly. If there are 50 questions, how many are answered correctly?

  A. 33   B. 35   C. 37   D. 39   E. 41

29. 42 % of the 2300 animals in a zoo are mammals. How many are not mammals?

   A.   920   B.   1120   C.   1304   D.   1334   E. 1920

30. In one day, 14 % of the flights from an airport are delayed. If there are 250 flights, how many take off on time?

   A.   100   B.   125   C.   205   D.   215   E. 23

5. Volume, Area and Perimeter

You need to be confident finding the area of squares, rectangles, triangles, parallelograms and compound shapes using these.

Remember....
Area is the measurement of a surface or piece of land ie the space it takes up.
Perimeter is the distance around the outside of a shape or piece of land.
Volume/Capacity is the amount of space enclosed within a container.

Example 1

A cuboid has a width of 7cm, height of 3cm and length of 5cm. What is its volume?
Solution : 7cm x 3cm x 5cm
Answer : 105cm^3

Example 2

Find the area of the triangle below.

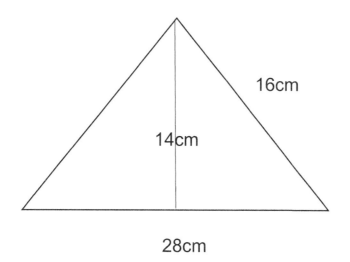

Solution A : (28cm x 14cm) ÷ 2

Answer : 196 cm^2

Solution B : (28 cm ÷ 2) x 14

Answer : 196 cm^2

1. A cuboid has a width of 8m, height of 5m and length of 12m. What is its volume in m³?

    A.   400 m³   B.   420 m³   C.   440 m³
    D.   460 m³   E.   480 m³

2. The edge of a cube is 6cm. What is its volume in cm³?

    A.   18 cm³   B.   36 cm³   C.   72 cm³
    D.   114 cm³   E.   216 cm³

3. The volume of a container is 640cm³. It has a width of 10cm and a height of 8cm. What is its length?

    A.   4cm   B.   6cm   C.   8cm   D.   9cm   E. 10cm

4. A large crate has a height of 12m, width of 8m and length of 16m. A smaller box has dimensions of : 4m height, 4m width and 4m length. How many small boxes will fit into the large crate?

    A.   12   B.   18   C.   20   D.   24   E. 28

5.

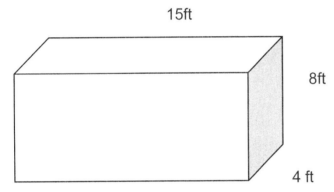

What is the volume of this cuboid in ft³?

    A.   480 ft³   B.   270 ft³   C.   240 ft³
    D.   524 ft³   E.   515 ft³

6. A tank is 4m long, 9m high and 0.5m in width. What is its volume?

    A.   9 m³   B.   18 m³   C.   27 m³
    D. 36 m³   E.   44 m³

7. A factory has a volume of 1944m^3. It has a height of 18m and a width of 12m. What is its length?

   A.   7m   B.   8m   C.   9m   D.   10m   E. 11m

8. A box of tissues has a length of 22cm, width of 12cm and height of 4cm. What is its volume?

   A.   1056 cm^3 B.   1508 cm^3 C.   880 cm^3
   D.   1236 cm^3 E.   960 cm^3

9. Box A has a height of 6cm, width of 4cm and length of 10cm. Box B has dimensions of: 2cm height, 2cm width and 2cm length. How many times can Crate B fit into Crate A?

   A.   26   B.   28   C.   30   D.   32   E. 34

10. The volume of a box is 240cm^3. Its width is 6cm, its height is 8cm. What is its length?

   A.   5cm   B.   11cm   C.   8cm   D.   12cm   E. 4cm

11. A vessel is 3m high, 5m wide and 11m long. What is its volume?

   A.   155m^3 B.   158m^3 C.   165m^3
   D.   180m^3 E.   195m^3

12.The edge of a cube is 9cm. What is its volume?

   A.   27cm^3 B.   81cm^3 C.   327cm^3
   D.   650cm^3 E.   729cm^3

13. A rectangle has a perimeter of 24cm. Which of these could be its area?
   A. 18cm^2 B.   26m^2 C.   29cm^2 D.   32cm^2 E. 40cm^2

14. If the area of a rectangle is 48 cm^2 and two of the sides measure 6 cm, what is the length of the other two sides?

   A.   12cm   B.   8cm   C.   7cm   D.   6cm   E.   4cm

15. I walk around a field three times. The length of the field is 200m and the width is 400m. How far have I walked in Km?

   A.   3.6 Km   B.   1.8 Km   C.   18 Km
   D.   1.2 Km   E.   36 Km

16.

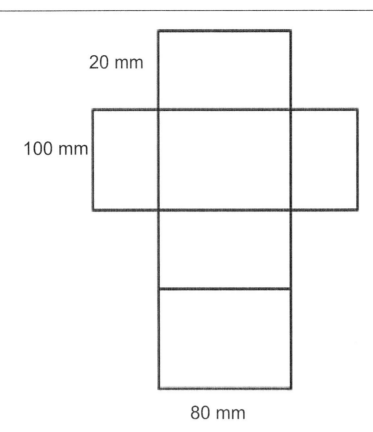

20 mm

100 mm

80 mm

What is the volume of the above cuboid in mm³?

  A.   16 000 mm³   B.   160 000 mm³   C.   200 000 mm³
  D.   216 000 mm³   E.   240 000 mm³

17.

B

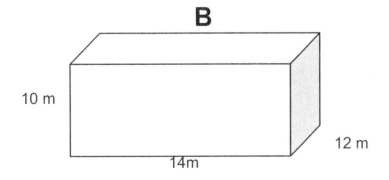

10 m

12 m

14m

A

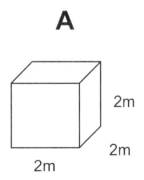

2m

2m

2m

How many of Box A will fit into Box B?

  A.   105   B.   125   C.   205   D.   210   E. 220

18.
          B   **A**

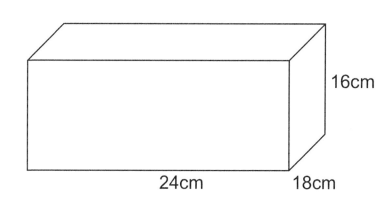 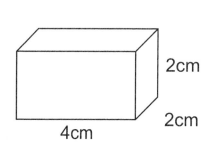

How many of Box A will fit into Box B?

A.   260   B.   384   C.   432   D.   486   E. 505

19.

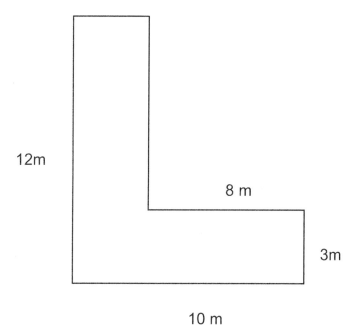

What is the area of the above shape?

A. $29m^2$ B. $36m^2$ C. $39m^2$ D. $44m^2$ E. $48m^2$

20. What is the perimeter of the above shape?

A.   29m   B.   35m   C.   38m   D.   44m   E. 47m

21.

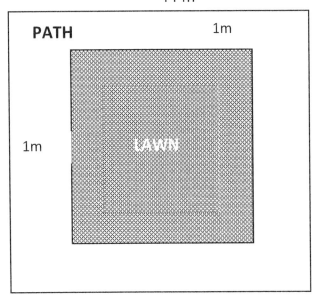

14 m

PATH   1m

1m   LAWN   12 m

What is the area of the lawn, if the path has a width of 1m all the way around the lawn?

A.   168m^2 B.   156m^2 C.   144m^2

D.   120m^2 E.   100m^2

22. In the above question, what is the perimeter of the lawn?

A. 52m   B.   48m   C.   44m   D.   26m   E. 22m

23. A square has an area of 121cm^2. What are the lengths of its sides?

A. 12cm   B.   11cm   C.   10cm   D.   9cm   E. 7cm

24. A rectangle has a perimeter of 30cm. Which of these could be its area?

A.   16cm^2 B.   25cm^2 C.   40cm^2

D.   50cm^2 E.   66cm^2

25.

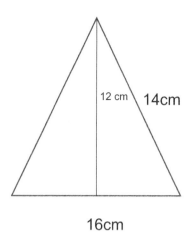

12 cm 14cm

16cm

What is the area of the triangle?

A.   224cm^2 B.   196cm^2

C.   192cm^2 D.   142cm^2

E.   96cm^2

26.

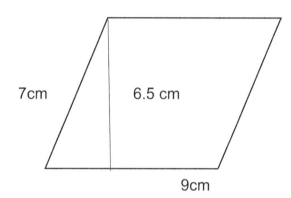

7cm   6.5 cm

9cm

What is the area of the parallelogram?

A.   63cm^2 B.   58.5cm^2 C.   46cm^2

D.   38.5cm^2 E.   32cm^2

27.

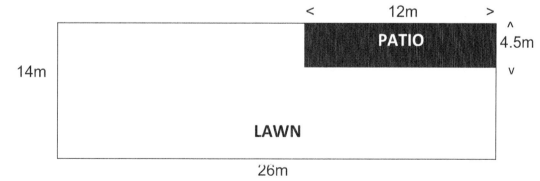

<   12m   >

PATIO   4.5m

14m

LAWN

26m

What is the area of the lawn?

A.   310 m^2 B.   378.5 m^2 C.   440.5 m^2 D.   302 m^2 E.   298 m^2

28.

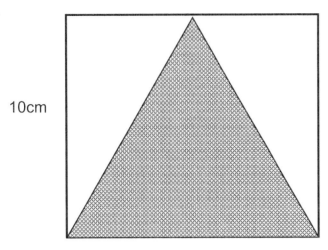

10cm

12cm

What is the area of the white section only of the above shape?

A.   48cm^2 B.   58cm^2 C.   60cm^2

D.   90cm^2 E.   120cm^2

29.

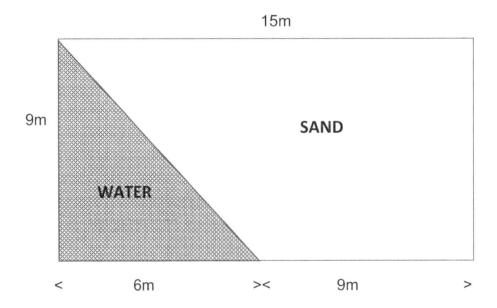

15m

9m

SAND

WATER

<   6m   ><   9m   >

What is the area of the sand shown on the diagram above?

A.   135m^2 B.   108m^2 C.   90m^2

D.   45m^2 E.   27m^2

30.

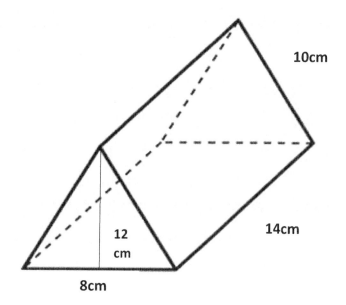

10cm

12 cm

14cm

8cm

What is the surface area of the triangular prism?

A.	96cm^2		B.	236cm^2	C.	376cm^2
D.	420cm^2		E.	516cm^2		

6. Ratio

Example One

A gardener plants **peas** and **beans** in a ratio of **1:2**. If **22** beans are planted how many peas are planted?

Peas : Beans   Beans = 22 ÷ 2 = 11   so we are multiplying by 11
   1 : 2   Therefore : Peas = 1 x 11 = 11
(X11)   (x11)
  11   22

Answer :   **11**

Example Two

Is similar to example one but take care to read the question CAREFULLY !

Suzie collects **teddy bears** and **china ornaments**. If she has a ratio of **3:1** and has **21** teddy bears, how many teddy bears and ornaments are there in **total**?

Bears : Ornaments   Bears = 21 ÷ 3 = 7   so we are multiplying by 7
   3 : 1
(x7)   (x7)
  21 : 7

The question asks how many bears and ornaments there are in TOTAL so
21 + 7 = 28

Answer :   **28**

Example 3

A gym has 90 members. The ratio of male to female members is 3 : 2.
How many members are female?

First : add the two parts of the ratio together	3 + 2 = 5
Next : divide the total number (90) by 5	90 ÷ 5 = 18
Finally : multiply the number of females in the ratio by 18	18 x 2 = 36

Answer :   **36**

Example 4

Simplifying ratios is the same as simplifying fractions. Find the highest factor of both numbers in the ratio.

Simplify   96 : 42
Both numbers are multiples of 6 so 96 ÷ 6 = 16
                                                    42 ÷ 6 = 7

Answer :   16:7

Remember always look carefully at the order of numbers in a ratio...7:4 is not the same as 4:7

Read the question and follow the order in the question. For example if the question says the ratio of boys to girls is 5:7 this means 5 parts are boys and 7 parts are girls.

1. A traffic survey records vehicles passing along a road. The ratio of cars to vans is 3:1. If 12 cars drive past, how many vans go by?

   A.   18   B.   6   C.   5   D.   4   E.   3

2. In a sports club the ratio of boys to girls is 5:7. If there are 49 girls, how many boys are there?

   A.   35   B.   33   C.   34   D.   32   E.   36

3. In a box of chocolates, there are 15 toffees. If the ratio of chocolates to toffees is 2:3, how many
     chocolates are there?

   A.   6   B.   10   C.   11   D.   12   E.   14

4. In a car park, there are blue and silver cars. If there are 72 silver cars and the ratio of silver to blue cars is 8:5, how many blue cars are there?

   A.   40   B.   45   C.   56   D.   65   E.   70

5. Amy, Bill and Charlotte share £160 between them in the ratio of 1:2:5. How much money does Bill receive?

   A.   £20   B.   £25   C.   £30   D.   £40   E.   £100

6. A farmer has 810 acres of land. He grows wheat, barley and corn in the ratio of 2:3:4. How many acres of corn does he grow?

   A.   180   B.   420   C.   520   D.   270   E.   360

7. A farmer has 1000 animals. He keeps pigs, cows and chickens in the ratio of 10:7:3. How many of the animals are cows?

A.   150   B.   350   C.   460   D.   500   E. 520

8. 90 people select a packet of crisps. They choose between salt and vinegar, bacon and plain in the ratio of 8:5:2. How many people chose salt and vinegar?

A.   12   B.   30   C.   48   D.   65   E. 70

9. Give 105:95 in its simplest form.

A.   19:21   B.   21:19   C.   20:9   D.   5:8   E. 7:13

10. Simplify 42:39

A.   17:13   B.   21:19   C.   21:19   D.   14:13   E. 7:6

11. Give the ratio 63:56 in its simplest form.

A.   9:8   B.   7:6   C.   8:9   D.   21:19   E. 6:7

12. Simplify 108:54

A.   8:5   B.   23:14   C.   11:5   D.   2:1   E. 7:9

13. Sophie used her mobile phone 132 times in a month for phone calls and texts, with a ratio of 7:4. How many texts does she send?

A.   48   B.   24   C.   12   D.   36   E.   60

14. A newsagent sells 108 comics and newspapers in a day, in a ratio of 3:9. How many newspapers does he sell in a day?

A.   63   B.   72   C.   81   D.   86   E.   90

15. A fish and chip shop sells fish and sausages in a ratio of 5:2. If they sell 63 items in total, how many portions of fish do they sell?

A.   10   B.   15   C.   30   D.   40   E.   45

16. A class has pens and pencils in a ratio of 2:3. If there are 60 pens and pencils in total, how many pencils are there?

A.   20   B.   28   C.   32   D.   36   E.   40

17. At Newtown Primary School 420 children walk to school. The ratio of those who cycle to walk is 3:7. How many children cycle to school?

   A.   120   B.   150   C.   180   D.   240   E.   300

18. In a music survey, the ratio of people who prefer pop music compared to classical music was 13:12. If 96 prefer classical, how many people prefer pop?

   A.   104   B.   100   C.   102   D.   98   E.   108

19. In an office, the ratio of right-handed people to left-handed is 8:5. If 24 people are right-handed, how many are left-handed?

   A.   10   B.   15   C.   18   D.   20   E.   22

20. On Saturday, a shoe shop sells 55 pairs of shoes. The ratio of shoes sold to boots sold is 5:6. How many pairs of boots are sold?

   A.   55   B.   44   C.   88   D.   77   E.   66

21. A restaurant has 54 tables and chairs in a ratio of 1:8. How many chairs are there?

   A.   16   B.   24   C.   32   D.   40   E.   48

22. An animal sanctuary has 104 animals. The ratio of horses to donkeys is 5:3. How many donkeys does it have?

   A.   33   B.   39   C.   46   D.   49   E.   54

23. A café sells 132 teas and coffees, in a ratio of 7:5. How many teas does it sell?

   A.   48   B.   60   C.   66   D.   77   E.   88

24. In a day, a postman delivers 170 items. The ratio of letters to parcels is 11:6. How many parcels are delivered?

   A.   60   B.   50   C.   40   D.   80   E.   70

25. A library lends fiction and non-fiction books, in a ratio of 20:14. In a day, 160 fiction books are borrowed. How many non-fiction books are borrowed?

   A.   94   B.   98   C.   102   D.   110   E.   112

26. A supermarket sells crisps and nuts in a ratio of 7:4. 84 packets of crisps are sold. How many packets of nuts are sold?

   A.   48   B.   50   C.   54   D.   58   E.   60

27. In a book, the ratio of pages of pictures to text is 2:5. There are 20 picture-pages. How many pages does the book have in total?

   A.   70   B.   35   C.   50   D.   40   E.   75

28. In a bouquet, the ratio of roses to carnations is 1:3. If there are 6 roses, how many flowers are in the bouquet in total?

   A.   9   B.   12   C.   18   D.   24   E.   30

29. There are 480 members in a bowls club. The ratio of over 60's to under 60's is 5:1. How many members are over 60?

   A.   420   B.   410   C.   400   D.   220   E.   80

30. Mrs Brown has 65 recipes in her cookbook. The ratio of cake recipes to biscuit recipes is 8:5. How many cake recipes are there?

   A.   26   B.   39   C.   40   D.   43   E.   49

31. £1200 is raised in a charity auction. It is divided between charities A, B and C in the ratio of 6:8:10. How much does charity A receive?

   A.   £550   B.   £500   C.   £400   D.   £360   E. £300

32. A football team plays 48 matches. The ratio of games won to lost is 9:7. How many games do they win?

   A.   29   B.   27   C.   21   D.   12   E.   6

33. In the word 'excellent', what is the ratio of vowels to consonants?

   A.   2:1   B.   3:5   C.   1:2   D.   2:7   E. 7:2

34. In the word 'examination', what is the ratio of consonants to vowels?

   A.   5:7   B.   6:5   C.   2:9   D.   5:6   E. 3:7

35. In a gallery, the ratio of oil to watercolour paintings is 180:420. Give this ratio in its simplest form.

   A.   9:17   B.   3:7   C.   6:13   D.   11:19   E. 7:3

36. In a greengrocers, the ratio of apples to pears is 84:21. Simplify this ratio.

   A.   1:4   B.   1:6   C.   6:1   D.   11:3   E. 4:1

37. In a football crowd, the ratio of those supporters wearing scarves to not wearing scarves is 264:96. Give this in its simplest form.

    A.   11:3   B.   17:13   C.   11:4   D.   4:11   E.   14:9

38. A takeaway sells pizzas and hotdogs in a ratio of 8:5. If 56 pizzas are sold, how many pizzas and hotdogs are sold altogether?

    A.   80   B.   85   C.   91   D.   106   E.   112

39. In a zoo, the ratio of zebras to elephants is 3:2. If there are 24 zebras, how many animals are there in total?

    A.   36   B.   40   C.   44   D.   50   E.   54

40. In a box of lego, the ratio of blue to red pieces is 4:3. If there are 480 blue pieces, how many pieces are there in total?

    A.   840   B.   910   C.   880   D.   950   E.   810

7. Measurements – Metric and Imperial

Example 1

A recipe contains the following ingredients: ½ kg of flour, 350g of butter,
¼ kg of sugar, 150g of cherries, 1/10 kg of almonds and 200g of sultanas.
What is their combined weight in Kg?

Solution:
Convert all ingredients to the same unit of measurement in this example grams.
Flour = 500g, sugar = 250g, almonds = 100g.
Add all the amounts together : 500 + 350 + 250 + 150 + 100 + 200 = 1550g
Convert into Kg by dividing by 1000.

Answer : 1.55 Kg

Example 2

Mrs. Richards is 5 feet 6 inches tall. What is her height in metres?

Solution:
Convert 5 feet 6 inches into inches. Multiply by 2.5 to convert into cm. Divide by 100
To convert into metres.

1 foot = 12 inches   therefore 5 feet = 60 inches + 6 inches = 66 inches
66 x 2.5 = 165cm ÷ 100 =

Answer: 1.65m

1. A piece of rope measure 6m 8cm. It is cut into two equal pieces. What is the length of each piece?

    A.   3.4 m   B.   3.04 m   C.   3m 40cm   D. 304 mm   E.   34 cm

2. I post three parcels. Parcel one weighs ½ Kg, parcel two weighs 800g and parcel three weighs 2.4 Kg. What is their combined weight?

    A.   7600 g   B.   0.37 Kg   C.   37 Kg   D.   730 g   E.   3.7 Kg

3. It is 0.6 Km to my school. Each day, I walk there and back. How far do I walk in one week?

    A.   3 Km   B.   300 m   C.   600 m   D.   6Km   E. 0.6Km

4. A bottle of juice contains 1.5 L. I pour out three glasses each containing 250ml. How much juice is left in the bottle?

A.   1000 ml   B.   800 ml   C.   0.75 L   D.   75 ml   E.   0.6 L

5. A field is 80 m long and 120 m wide. In the school cross-country, I run around it three times. How far have I run?

A.   400 m   B.   0.8 Km   C.   1 Km   D.   1.2 Km   E.   12 Km

6. A recipe uses: 150 g of butter, ½ Kg of flour and 150 g of sugar. What is the combined weight of these ingredients?

A.   1300 g   B.   1 Kg   C.   0.95 Kg   D.   0.8 Kg   E.   750 g

7. A ribbon is divided into 4 equal pieces and cut. The whole ribbon measures 404cm. How long is each piece?

A.   2.2 m   B.   110 cm   C.   44 cm   D.   100 cm   E.   1.01 m

8. A bucket can hold 6 L, when full. It is now ¾ full. How much liquid is in the bucket?

A.   1500 ml   B.   3 L   C.   1.5 L   D.   4.5 L   E.   45 L

9. Lily's school bag weighs 1.25 Kg. Her sister's bag weighs 1680 g. What is the difference between them?

A.   2.93 Kg   B.   0.8 Kg   C.   750 g   D.   0.43 Kg   E.   4.3 Kg

10. Mike drives to work each day. He travels 4.25 Km each way. How far does he travel in one week?

A.   425 m   B.   4 Km   C.   4250 m   D.   42.5 Km   E.   425 Km

11. Mrs. Brown is 5 feet 4 inches tall. Which of these is closest to her height in metres?

A.   1.4 m   B.   1.5 m   C.   1.6 m   D.   1.8 m   E.   2 m

12. Angie is 4 feet 11 inches tall. Which is closest to her height in metres?

A.   1.5 m   B.   1.7 m   C.   1.8 m   D.   1.9 m   E.   2 m

13. 1 Km is approximately 0.6 miles. Bill travels 8 Km. Approximately, how many miles has he travelled?

A.   3   B.   4   C.   5   D.   6   E.   7

14. The distance from London to Bath is 115 miles. Approximately, what is this distance measured
    in Kilometres?

A.   124   B.   135   C.   156   D.   184   E.   200

15. A door frame is 1.8 m high. Approximately what is this measured in inches?

A.   66   B.   60   C.   80   D.   76   E.   71

16.

Fl Ounces	Ml
1	28.4
2	56.8
3	?
4	113.6

The above table converts fluid ounces into ml. What is the missing measurement?

A.   68.4   B.   76.6   C.   85.2   D.   90.4   E. 98.6

17.

Pounds (lbs)	Kg
5	2.27
6	2.72
7	3.18
8	?

The above table converts pounds into Kilograms. What is the missing measurement?
A.   3.28   B.   3.63   C.   3.94   D.   4.02   E. 4.12

18.

Celsius	Fahrenheit
20	68
21	69.8
22	71.6
23	?

The above table converts degrees celsius into degrees fahrenheit. Complete the table.

A.   72.8°   B.   73.1°   C.   73.4°   D.   74.2°   E. 74.8°

19.

Yards	Metres (to 2dp)
4	3.66
5	?
6	5.49
7	6.4

The above table converts yards into metres (rounded to 2 decimal places). Complete the table.

A.   3.98   B.   4.07   C.   4.57   D.   4.94   E. 5.14

20. Which of these measurements is closest to the average capacity of a bath?

A.   30 L   B.   3 L   C.   3000 L   D.   1000 L   E. 300 L

21. Which of these measurements is closest to the weight of an average sized apple?

A.   9 g   B.   90 g   C.   200 g   D.   0.5 Kg   E.   1000 g

22. Which of these measurements is closest to the height of an average door?

A.   1.2 m   B.   1.4 m   C.   140 cm   D.   2 m   E.   400 cm

23. Which of these measurements is closest to the capacity of an average sized mug?

A.   350 ml   B.   800 ml   C.   0.8 L   D. 1.5 L   E.   2000 ml

24. Which of these measurements is closest to the weight of an average size schoolbag?

A.   6 Kg   B.   1 Kg   C.   3000 g   D.   20 Kg   E.   9000 g

25. Which of these measurements is closest to the length of an average pencil?

A.   10 mm   B.   50 mm   C.   18 cm D.   30 cm   E. 0.3 m

26. Which of these measurements is closest to the capacity of an average sink?

A.   6 L   B.   7000 ml   C.   16 L   D.   1.6 L   E. 50 L

27. What is the difference between 13.4 L and 8.25 L?

A.   6.15 L   B.   5950 ml   C.   5.1 L   D.   5000 ml   E. 5150 ml

28. What is the total weight of 75g, 0.086Kg and 143 g?

A.   300 g   B.   0.304 Kg   C.   305 g   D.   0.35 Kg   E. 350 g

29. What is the difference between 3.4 cm and 7.6 cm?

   A.   4.1 cm   B.   0.4 cm   C.   42 mm   D.   4.5 cm   E. 48 mm

30. Mr. Richards grows an enormous pumpkin weighing 10.4 Kg. He cuts it into slices and shares it with 7 friends. How much does each person receive?

   A.   130 g   B.   1.1 Kg   C.   1250 g   D.   1300 g   E.   1.03 Kg

8. Averages

Mean: add all the numbers then divide by how many numbers there are.
Mode: the most frequently occurring number
Median: the number in the middle, once the data has been put in ascending order
Range: is not an average. It is the difference between the highest and lowest numbers in the data. If the question asks you to find the average but does not state which to use, always calculate the mean.

Example

Mr Harvey records the number of birds visiting his garden each day for a week.

Mon	Tues	Weds	Thurs	Fri	Sat	Sun
12	8	15	9	16	12	5

a) What is the mean amount?
Solution: 12 + 8 + 15 + 9 + 16 + 12 + 5 = 77 ÷ 7 =
Answer: 11

b) What is the mode?
Answer: 12

c) What is the median?
Solution: 5 8 9 **12** 12 15 16
Answer: 12

d) What is the range?
Solution: 16 – 5
Answer: 11

1. Mike records the number of biscuits he eats in a week.

Mon	Tues	Weds	Thurs	Fri	Sat	Sun
3	2	5	1	4	3	3

a)   What is the mean amount he eats?

   A.   1   B.   2   C.   3   D.   4   E.   5

b)   What is the range?

   A.   4   B.   2   C.   1   D.   3   E.   5

2. A shop sells papers every weekday.

Mon	Tues	Weds	Thurs	Fri
80	72	88	96	104

a)   What is the average amount sold?

   A.   90   B.   88   C.   82   D.   72   E.   68

b)   What is the median amount?

   A.   96   B.   88   C.   80   D.   72   E.   68

3. Mrs Brown drinks tea every day. She records the number of cups each weekday.

Mon	Tues	Weds	Thurs	Fri
5	2	3	4	?

If her mean is 4. How many cups did she drink on Friday?

   A.   11   B.   9   C.   6   D.   5   E.   4

4. These are Andy's spelling scores over a 6 week period.

Week 1	Week 2	Week 3	Week 4	Week 5	Week 6
19	17	20	17	18	17

a)   What is his mean score?

   A.   16   B.   17   C.   18   D.   19   E.   20

b)   What is the modal score?

   A.   17   B.   18   C.   19   D.   20   E.   21

c)   What is his range?

   A.   0   B.   1   C.   2   D.   3   E.   4

d)   What is the median score?

   A.   17   B.   17.5   C.   18   D.   18.5   E.   19

5. Sophie records the amount of time spent on homework, in minutes, each day

Mon	Tues	Weds	Thurs	Fri	Sat	Sun
45	30	60	50	30	70	100

a)   What is the average amount of time she spends on homework per day, in minutes?

   A.   88   B.   77   C.   66   D.   55   E.   44

b)   What is the modal amount of time spent, in minutes?

   A.   30   B.   45   C.   50   D.   70   E. 100

c)   What is the median, in minutes?

   A.   30   B.   45   C.   50   D.   60   E. 100

6. A radio station records how many songs it plays each day.

Mon	Tues	Weds	Thurs	Fri	Sat	Sun
240	212	202	250	290	310	295

a)   What is the average number of songs it plays?

   A.   247   B.   257   C.   266   D.   284   E. 287

b)   What is the range?

   A.   93   B.   98   C.   108   D.   112   E. 114

c)   What is the median?

   A.   250   B.   290   C.   295   D.   302   E. 310

7. Chris is training for a marathon. He runs the following number of miles over a week.

Mon	Tues	Weds	Thurs	Fri	Sat	Sun
8	7	10	14	18	?	22

He calculates his mean is 14. How many miles did he run on Saturday?

   A.   24   B.   19   C.   17   D.   14   E.   12

8. A class record the amount of rainfall, in mm, over a 12-month period. The results are shown below.

Jan	Feb	Mar	Apr	May	Jun	Jul	Aug	Sep	Oct	Nov	Dec
50	47	43	34	20	14	6	?	20	42	60	66

The mean amount each month is calculated as 34 mm.
How many mm fell in August?

A.   14   B.   12   C.   4   D.   10   E.   6

9. In 10 days Eric watches the following amount of television each day, recorded in minutes.

Day	1	2	3	4	5	6	7	8	9	10
Mins	100	65	80	20	120	35	45	110	180	?

His mean is 80 minutes.
How many minutes does he watch on Day 10?

A.   20   B.   25   C.   35   D.   40   E.   45

10. Mrs Smith grows strawberries. She picks some each day for 9 days.

Day	1	2	3	4	5	6	7	8	9
Number picked	10	14	?	7	11	9	16	6	18

The mean she picks each day is 11.
How many strawberries does she pick on day 3?

A.   8   B.   9   C.   10   D.   12   E.   14

11. Four friends compare their pocket money each week.

Amy	Beth	Freya	Ellen
£3.50	£2.50	£3.25	£3.75

a) What is the average amount of pocket money received?

A.   £2.75   B.   £3.00   C.   £3.25   D.   £3.40   E. £3.50

b) What is the range?

A.   £0.25   B.   £0.50   C.   £0.75   D.   £1.00   E. £1.25

12. A dice is rolled 20 times. The number thrown each time is shown below.

3	2	4	6	2	4	2	6	1	3
5	3	5	6	2	1	5	4	3	2

What is the modal number thrown?

A.   2   B.   3   C.   4   D.   5   E.   6

13. Three friends buy items at the school tuck shop. The table below shows the amount they spend.

Tom	Ben	Sam
£2.15	£1.85	£2.45

a) What is the mean amount they spend?

A.   £0.60   B.   £1.45   C.   £2.25
D.   £2.05   E.   £2.15

14. Ellen and her three friends pick raspberries. The amount picked by each person is shown below in Kg.

Ellen	Claire	Grace	Emily
2.1 Kg	1.8 Kg	2.3 Kg	1.6 Kg

a) What is the mean amount picked, in Kg, to two decimal places?

A.   1.75   B.   1.82   C.   1.87   D.   1.95   E.   2.04

b) What is the range of weights?

A.   500 g   B.   600 g   C.   650 g
D.   700 g   E.   850 g

15. A shoe shop sells the following size shoes on a Saturday.

5	6	2	4	6	8	7	2	3	5	4	5	7	2	5

What is the modal size?

A.   2   B.   4   C.   5   D.   7   E.   8

16. Test scores are compared by 8 students. The results are shown in the table below.

Student	1	2	3	4	5	6	7	8
Maths %	64	83	58	52	77	90	72	68
English %	75	86	70	56	71	82	58	66

a) What is the mean % score for Maths?

A. 70.5   B. 68.5   C. 64   D. 70   E. 75

b) What is the mean % score for English?

A. 64   B. 68.5   C. 70   D. 70.5   E. 75

c) What is the range for Maths?

A. 13   B. 21   C. 31   D. 38   E. 40

d) What is the range for English?

A. 15   B. 26   C. 20   D. 32   E. 30

e) What is the median score for Maths?

A. 68   B. 70   C. 72   D. 83   E. 90

f) What is the median score for English?

A. 58   B. 66   C. 68.5   D. 70   E. 70.5

17. The points scored whilst playing a game are recorded in the table below.

42	37	41	50	38	41	36	54	67	44

a) What is the modal score?

A. 36   B. 38   C. 41   D. 42   E. 50

b) What is the range of scores?

A. 18   B. 22   C. 27   D. 31   E. 35

c) What is the mean score?

A. 54   B. 49   C. 45   D. 41   E. 39

18. Six friends grow sunflowers and measure them when fully grown. The heights are recorded below in cm.

159	180	164	137	168	173

a) What is the average height of the sunflowers, in cm?

A.　180　B.　170　C.　165.5　D.　163.5　E.　162

b) What is the median height, in cm?

A.　164　B.　165.5　C.　166　D.　168　E.　180

c) What is the range of heights, in cm?

A.　43　B.　36　C.　31　D.　25　E.　5

19. Alice records her house-points over a 12- week term.

7	4	6	5	8	12	6	7	5	7	11	12

a) What is her mean amount?

A.　6　B.　6.5　C.　7　D.　7.5　E.　9

b) What is the modal amount?

A.　5　B.　6　C.　7　D.　8　E.　10

c) What is the median amount?

A.　5　B.　7　C.　8　D.　11　E.　12

d) What is the range?

A.　6　B.　7　C.　8　D.　9　E.　10

20. Simon and his two brothers record the amount of time they spend on their I-pad each day for one week. The time is recorded in minutes.

Simon	22	28	31	26	35	40	42
Mike	18	26	21	14	39	47	50
Paul	17	30	25	23	30	44	48

a) What is the mean amount of time Simon spends on his I-pad, in minutes?

A.   26   B.   28   C.   30   D.   32   E.   38

b) What is the mode for Paul?

A.   23   B.   25   C.   30   D.   32   E.   44

c) What is the difference between Mike's range of time and Simon's range of time?

A.   5   B.   9   C.   16   D.   17   E.   20

9. 2D and 3D Shapes and Angles

All the 3D shapes below will be used in questions in this section.

Key Points to Learn

Be familiar with 2D and 3D shape properties ie the number of faces, edges and vertices of the shapes below.

Also, the number of sides, lines of symmetry and order of rotational symmetry of common 2D shapes ie all quadrilaterals, triangles, hexagons, octagons, decagons, nonagons, heptagons, pentagons.

Understand what is meant by a regular shape. Learn the total interior angles of quadrilaterals, triangles and the number of degrees on a straight line and therefore be able to calculate missing angles.

3D Shapes

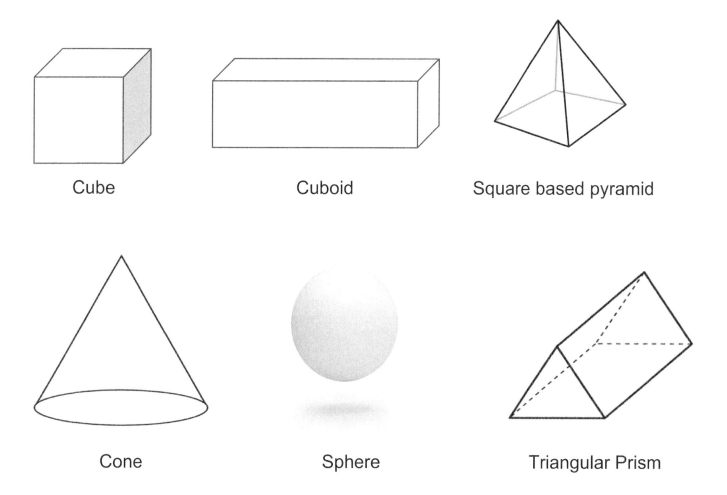

Cube   Cuboid   Square based pyramid

Cone   Sphere   Triangular Prism

1. How many vertices does a triangular prism have?

   A.   5   B.   6   C.   7   D.   8   E.   12

2. How many vertices does a cube have?

   A.   6   B.   12   C.   9   D.   10   E.   8

3. How many vertices does a cone have?

   A.   0   B.   1   C.   2   D.   3   E.   4

4. How many vertices does a square based pyramid have?

   A.   1   B.   4   C.   5   D.   6   E.   8

5. How many faces does a cuboid have?

   A.   3   B.   4   C.   5   D.   6   E.   8

6. How many faces does a cylinder have?

   A.   1   B.   2   C.   3   D.   5   E.   6

7. How many faces does a sphere have?

   A.   0   B.   1   C.   2   D.   3   E.   4

8. How many edges does a cube have?

   A.   8   B.   9   C.   12   D.   14   E.   15

9. How many edges does a triangular prism have?

   A.   6   B.   7   C.   8   D.   9   E.   12

10. How many edges does a cone have?

   A.   1   B.   2   C.   8   D.   9   E.   12

11. Which of these shapes have the same number of vertices?

    A.   cube and cuboid   B.   cube and triangular prism

    C.   cone and sphere   D.   square based pyramid and triangular prism

    E.   cuboid and square based pyramid

12. Which of these shapes have the same number of faces?

    A.   cube and sphere   B.   cone and cylinder

    C.   triangular prism and square based pyramid   D.   cone and sphere

    E.   cuboid and triangular prism

13. How many lines of symmetry does a regular hexagon have?

    A.   2   B.   3   C.   4   D.   6   E.   12

14. How many lines of symmetry does a regular decagon have?

    A.   6   B.   8   C.   10   D.   12   E.   20

15. What is the order of rotational symmetry of an equilateral triangle?

    A.   2   B.   0   C.   5   D.   4   E.   3

16. How many pairs of parallel lines does a parallelogram have?

    A.   0   B.   1   C.   2   D.   3   E.   4

17. How many lines of symmetry does a kite have?

    A.   0   B.   1   C.   2   D.   3   E.   4

18. How many lines of symmetry does a parallelogram have?

    A.   0   B.   1   C.   2   D.   3   E.   4

19. What is the order of rotational symmetry of a rhombus?

    A.   1   B.   2   C.   3   D.   4   E.   5

20. Find the missing angle, marked x, in the shape below.

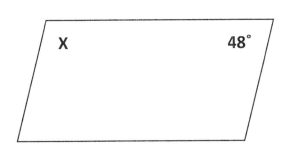

(Angles not drawn accurately)

A.   48°   B.   68°   C.   96°   D.   132°   E.   142°

21. Find the missing angle, marked x, in the shape below.

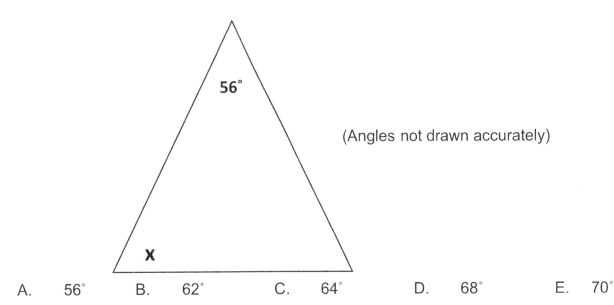

(Angles not drawn accurately)

A.   56°   B.   62°   C.   64°   D.   68°   E.   70°

22. What is the name of the triangle with no equal sides or angles?

A.   equilateral   B.   isosceles   C.   trapezium

D.   scalene   E.   regular

23.   Which of these is a reflex angle?

A.   187°   B.   142°   C.   136°   D.   165°   E.   97°

24. What is the difference in sides between a nonagon and a pentagon?

A.   1   B.   2   C.   3   D.   4   E.   5

25. If one angle on a straight line is shown as 34°, what would the other angle measure?

    A.   158°   B.   116°   C.   128°   D.   90°   E.   146°

26. The interior angles of a quadrilateral always total how many degrees?

    A.   100°   B.   180°   C.   200°   D.   240°   E.   360°

27. Which of these shapes has 2 lines of symmetry and an order of rotational symmetry of 2?

    A.   kite   B.   square   C.   trapezium   D. rectangle
    E.   parallelogram

28. How many pairs of parallel sides does a trapezium have?

    A.   0   B.   1   C.   2   D.   3   E.   4

29. Which of the answers below shows an acute angle, obtuse angle and reflex angle?

	Acute	Obtuse	Reflex
A	12°	94°	100°
B	47°	136°	196°
C	91°	106°	150°
D	54°	83°	235°
E	68°	77°	342°

30. A scalene triangle has angles of 47°, 63° and x°. What is the size of angle x?

    A.   65°   B.   68°   C.   70°   D.   75°   E.   80°

10. General number questions-

Including inverse calculations, square, cube, triangle and prime numbers, multiples and reasoning

Key points

Learn all square numbers upto 12^2 (1, 4, 9, 16, 25, 36, 49, 64, 81, 100, 121 , 144)
Learn cube numbers to 5^3. (1, 8, 27, 64, 125)
Learn what a prime number is – a number that can only be divided by 1 and itself to give a whole number as the answer.
Be familiar with the triangle number pattern (1, 3, 6, 10, 15, 21, 28 ....)
Understand that inverse means the opposite of an operation ie subtraction is the inverse of addition, division is the inverse of multiplication.
Multiples are the product of given numbers eg the 5th multiple of 9 is 45.
Use reasoning skills to help solve problems eg 15 x 13 = 195 so 1.5 x 1.3 = 1.95

1. I think of a number, treble it, add 2 and then subtract 6. My answer is 17. What number did I start with?

   A. 3   B.   7   C.   21   D.   27   E.   29

2. I think of a number, double it, divide by 4 and then multiply by 5. My answer is 30. What number did I start with?

   A. 3   B.   6   C.   12   D.   24   E.   48

3. I think of a number, divide it by 3, add 5 and then multiply by 6. My answer is 72. What number did I start with?

   A. 20   B.   21   C.   24   D.   33   E.   46

4. I think of a number, multiply it by 4, divide by 12 and then divide by 3. My answer is 1. What number did I start with?

   A. 9   B.   12   C.   16   D.   18   E.   20

5. I think of a number, subtract 5, divide by 5 and then multiply by 8. My answer is 24. What number did I start with?

   A.   10   B.   15   C.   20   D.   25   E.   25

6. I think of a number, add 6, double the answer and then divide by 8. My answer is 5. What number did I start with?

   A. 14   B.   24   C.   26   D.   36   E.   86

7. I think of a number, take 7 away, add 4 and then quarter it. My answer is 3. What number did I start with?

A.   8   B.   9   C.   15   D.   18   E.   21

8. I think of a number, divide it by 5, increase it by 3 and then multiply by 6. My answer is 60. What number did I start with?

   A. 15   B.   24   C.   30   D.   33   E.   35

9. I think of a number, add 9, divide by 5 and then multiply by 15. My answer is 120. What number did I start with?

   A.   21   B.   24   C.   27   D.   31   E.   49

10. I think of a number, increase it by 12, multiply by 12 and then subtract 1. My answer is 203. What number did I start with?

   A. 1   B.   2   C.   3   D.   4   E.   5

11. I think of a number, divide it by 6, treble it and then add 7. My answer is 28. What number did I start with?

   A. 24   B.   42   C.   60   D.   72   E.   111

12. I think of a number, multiply it by 11, add 8 and then halve it. My answer is 15. What number did I start with?

   A.   0   B.   1   C.   2   D.   4   E.   5

13. I think of a number, square it, subtract 6 and then multiply by 11. My answer is 330. What number did I start with?

   A. 12   B.   10   C.   9   D.   8   E.   6

14. I think of a number, quarter it, multiply by 6 and then add 7. My answer is 367. What number did I start with?

   A. 120   B.   240   C.   280   D.   360   E.   384

15. I think of a number, decrease by 6, double it and then add 8. My answer is 70. What number did I start with?

    A. 25   B.   33   C.   37   D.   130   E.   150

16. I think of a number, reduce it by 8, multiply by 5 and then halve. My answer is 25. What number did I start with?

    A.   9   B.   12   C.   16   D.   18   E.   20

17. I think of a number, halve it, add 3 and then divide by 9. My answer is 6. What number did I start with?

    A. 88   B.   94   C.   100   D.   102   E. 114

18. I think of a number, treble it, square it and then add 4. My answer is 40. What number did I start with?

    A. 2   B.   3   C.   4   D.   15   E.   18

19. I think of a number, add 1, multiply by 1 and then add 8. My answer is 9. What number did I start with?

    A. 0   B.   1   C.   2   D.   4   E.   7

20. I think of a number, add 4, divide by 10 and then treble. My answer is 27. What number did I start with?

    A.   76   B.   85   C.   86   D.   92   E.   94

21. Which answer contains a square number, multiple of 9 and a cube number?

	Square number	Multiple of 9	Cube number
A	36	36	36
B	49	18	9
C	4	54	27
D	101	99	108
E	15	108	64

22. Which answer contains a square number, prime number and a cube number?

	Square number	Prime number	Cube number
A	16	7	6
B	21	11	27
C	49	13	8
D	99	24	9
E	36	18	15

23. Which answer contains a square number, prime number and a cube number?

	Square number	Prime number	Cube number
A	8	3	64
B	25	1	100
C	121	14	12
D	50	26	88
E	64	2	125

24. Which answer contains a square number, triangle number and a prime number?

	Square number	Triangle number	Prime number
A	4	1	12
B	81	4	13
C	38	9	82
D	100	15	17
E	144	24	9

25. Which answer contains a square number, triangle number and a prime number?

	Square number	Triangle number	Prime number
A	65	28	20
B	9	21	19
C	49	40	31
D	36	18	29
E	1	6	24

26. Which answer contains a multiple of 3, multiple of 7 and multiple of 8?

	Multiple of 3	Multiple of 7	Multiple of 8
A	12	49	96
B	33	22	18
C	29	56	64
D	15	14	41
E	274	36	80

27. Which answer contains a multiple of 4, multiple of 6 and multiple of 5?

	Multiple of 4	Multiple of 6	Multiple of 5
A	16	12	21
B	40	19	25
C	28	44	45
D	21	36	80
E	24	72	90

28. If (32 x 24) – 80 = 688

   Which of the following is incorrect?

   A. 32 x 24 = 688 + 80   B.   688 = (32 x 24) – 80

   C. -80 = 688 – (32 x 24)   D.   (32 x 24) – 81 = 687

   E. 32 (24 – 80) = 688

29. If (27 x 38) + 24 = 1050

   Which of the following is incorrect?

   A. 24 = 1050 – (27 x 38)   B.   1050 – 24 = (27 x 38)

   C. (27 x 38) + 25 = 1049   D.   27 x 38 = 1050 – 24

   E. (27 x 38) + 26 = 1052

30. If 758 = (18 x 43) – 16

   Which of the following is incorrect?

   A. 758 + 16 = 18 x 43   B.   (18 x 43) – 16 = 758

   C. 757 = (18 x 43) – 17   D.   758 – 16 = 18 x 43

   E. 759 = (18 x 43) - 15

11. Scale

Example 1

The scale on a map is 1:420000. What actual distance in Km is represented by 4cm on the map?

Solution:

1cm = 420,000cm
Divide by 100,000 to convert into Km as 100,000cm = 1Km
420,000 ÷ 100,000 = 4.2 Km
Multiply 4.2 by 4 =
Answer: 16.8 Km

Example 2
The scale on a map is 1:175000. How many cm on the map is equal to 42 Km?

Solution:
175,000 ÷ 100,000 = 1.75 Km = 1cm
42 ÷ 1.75 =
Answer: 24cm

Example 3

A plan of a garden has a scale of 1cm:3.5m. If the length of the garden is 28m. What is the length on the plan?

Solution:
Divide the length of the garden by 3.5 to convert into cm
28 ÷ 3.5 =
Answer: 8cm

1. The scale on a map is 1:250000. What actual distance, in Km, is represented by 3 cm on the map?

   A. 0.75Km   B.   7.5Km   C.   75Km   D.   750Km   E.   7500Km

2. The scale on a map is 1:120000. What actual distance is represented by 5 cm on the map?

   A. 600Km   B.   60Km   C.   600m   D.   0.6Km   E.   6Km

3. The scale on a map is 1:375000. What actual distance, in Km, is represented by 8 cm on the map?

   A. 30Km   B.   300Km   C.   3000Km   D.   3Km   E.   0.3Km

4. The scale on a map is 1:145000. What actual distance, in Km, is represented by 6 cm on the map?

   A. 8700Km   B.   870Km   C.   87Km   D.   8.7Km   E.   0.87Km

5. The scale on a map is 1:600000. What actual distance, in Km, is represented by 0.5 cm on the map?

   A. 30000Km   B.   3000Km   C.   300Km   D.   30Km   E.   3Km

6. A plan of a house is drawn using a scale of 1cm:3m. If the length of a room on the plan is 4.5cm, what is the actual length of the room?

   A. 9m   B.   12m   C.   13.5m   D.   15.5m   E. 18m

7. A plan of a playground has a scale of 1cm:5m. If the length of the playground on the plan is 8cm, what is the actual length of the playground?

   A. 10m   B.   20m   C.   30m   D.   40m   E. 50m

8. The plan of a field is drawn using a scale of 2cm:20m. If the width of the field on the plan is 12cm, what is its actual width?

   A. 120m   B.   100m   C.   80m   D.   180m   E. 140m

9. A plan of a garden has a scale of 1cm:2.5m. If the length of the garden is 12.5m, what is the length on the plan?

   A. 6.5cm   B.   6cm   C.   5.5cm   D.   5cm   E. 4cm

10. The plan of a warehouse has a scale of 1cm:3m. If the width of the warehouse is 18m, what is the width on the plan?

    A. 2cm   B.   4cm   C.   6cm   D.   8cm   E. 10cm

11. The scale on a map is 1:275000. How many cm on the map are equal to 55Km?

    A.   27.5cm   B.   25cm   C.   20cm   D.   18.5cm   E. 15cm

12. The scale on a map is 1:350000. How many cm on the map are equal to 42Km?

    A.   18cm   B.   16cm   C.   14cm   D.   12cm   E. 10cm

13. The scale on a map is 1:180000. How many cm on the map are equal to 9Km?

A.   9cm   B.   8cm   C.   7cm   D.   6cm   E. 5cm

14. The scale on a map is 1:240000. How many cm on the map are equal to 96Km?

A.   40cm   B.   36cm   C.   28cm   D.   24cm   E. 20cm

15. The scale on a map is 1:420000. How many cm on the map are equal to 63Km?

A. 5cm   B.   10cm   C.   15cm   D.   20cm   E. 20cm

16. The scale on a map is 1:160000. What actual distance, in Km, is represented by 4cm?

A. 5.6Km   B.   5.9Km   C.   6.1Km   D.   6.4Km   E.   6.7Km

17. The scale on a map is 1:230000. What actual distance, in Km, is represented by 7cm?

A.   21Km   B.   20.1Km   C.   19.3Km   D. 16.1Km   E.   15.7Km

18.   The scale on a map is 1:380000. What actual distance, in Km, is represented by 3cm?

A. 12Km   B.   11.4Km   C.   10.5Km   D.   9Km   E.   8.7Km

19. The scale on a map is 1:195000. What actual distance, in Km, is represented by 5cm?

A. 10Km   B.   9.75Km   C.   9.5Km   D.   9.25Km   E.   9Km

20. The scale on a map is 1:245000. What actual distance, in Km, is represented by 8cm?

A. 19.6Km   B.   18.6Km   C.   16.8Km   D.   19.8Km   E.   20.8Km

21. The scale on a map is 1:210000. How many cm on the map are equal to 210Km?

A.   1000cm   B.   500cm   C.   100cm   D. 50cm   E.   10cm

22. The scale on a map is 1:375000. How many cm on the map are equal to 15Km?

A.   3cm   B.   3.5cm C.   3.7cm   D.   4cm   E. 4.7cm

23. The scale on a map is 1:450000. How many cm on the map are equal to 81Km?

A.   9cm   B.   26cm   C.   12cm   D.   22cm   E. 18cm

24. The scale on a map is 1:175000. How many cm on the map are equal to 21Km?

A.   17.5cm   B.   15.5cm   C.   14cm   D.   12cm   E. 10cm

25. The scale on a map is 1:540000. How many cm on the map are equal to 27Km?

   A.   8cm   B.   7cm   C.   6cm   D.   5cm   E.   4cm

26. A plan of a football pitch has a scale of 1cm:12.5m. If the length of the football pitch on the plan is 9cm, what is the actual length?

   A.   100m   B.   110m   C.   112.5m   D.   115m   E.   118.5m

27. The plan of a sports hall has a scale of 2cm:8m. If the hall is 5cm long on the plan, what is the actual length of the hall?

   A.   15cm   B.   20cm   C.   25cm   D.   30cm   E.   35cm

28. A plan of a netball court has a scale of 1cm:5.5m. If the court is 27.5m long, what is the length on the plan?

   A.   3cm   B.   3.5cm   C.   4cm   D.   4.5cm   E   5cm

29. A plan of a house has a scale of 0.5cm:2m. if the hall is 6m long, what is the length of the hall on the plan?

   A.   1cm   B.   1.25cm   C.   1.5cm   D.   1.75cm   E   2cm

30. A plan of forest has a scale of 2cm:20m. If the forest is 50m wide, what is the width on the plan?

   A.   5cm   B.   5.5cm   C.   6cm   D.   8cm   E   8.5cm

12. Algebra

Finding the value of x, substitution, writing and using expressions, identifying incorrect statements, finding the nth term and the mean

Finding the value of x

Example

If $2x + 14 = 6x + 6$. Find the value of x.

$$14 - 6 = 6x - 2x$$
$$8 = 4x$$
$$2 = x$$

Answer: x=2

1. If $3x - 6 = 5x - 12$. Find the value of x.

   A.   1   B.   2   C.   3   D.   4   E.   5

2. If $8x + 10 = 4x + 30$. Find the value of x.

   A.   4   B.   5   C.   6   D.   7   E.   8

3. If $9x - 4 = 2x + 17$. Find the value of x.

   A.   3   B.   5   C.   7   D.   9   E.   11

4. If $x + 8 = 7x - 40$. Find the value of x.

   A.   5   B.   6   C.   7   D.   8   E.   9

5. If $-3x + 5 = 2x - 25$. Find the value of x.

   A.   2   B.   3   C.   4   D.   5   E.   6

6. If $2x + 2 = -10x + 26$. Find the value of x.

   A.   1   B.   2   C.   3   D.   4   E.   5

7. If $20x + 4 = 13x + 32$. Find the value of x.

   A.   2   B.   3   C.   4   D.   6   E.   8

8. If $21x - 18 = 19x - 4$. Find the value of x.

   A.   2   B.   3   C.   5   D.   7   E.   10

9. If $-2x - 10 = x - 13$. Find the value of x.

   A.   1   B.   3   C.   5   D.   7   E.   9

10. If $4x - 1 = 6x - 9$. Find the value of x

   A.   2   B.   3   C.   4   D.   6   E.   8

11. If $15x + 7 = x + 105$. Find the value of x.

   A.   1   B.   2   C.   4   D.   6   E.   7

12. If $-8x + 43 = 13x + 1$. Find the value of x.

   A.   2   B.   4   C.   6   D.   8   E.   10

13. If $3x + 5 = -9x + 65$. Find the value of x.

   A.   2   B.   3   C.   5   D.   7   E.   12

14. If $4x + 10 = -4x + 90$. Find the value of x.

   A.   4   B.   7   C.   9   D.   10   E.   15

15. If $14x - 10 = 4x + 110$. Find the value of x.

   A.   2   B.   4   C.   6   D.   8   E.   12

Identifying incorrect statements

Example

If $4x + 6y = 8z$. Which of the following is incorrect?

A.	$8x + 12y = 16z$	Correct.	Everything has been doubled.
B.	$2x + 3y = 4z$	Correct.	Everything has been halved.
C.	$4x + 6y - 8z = 0$	Correct.	If both sides are = then subtracting 1 side from the other must equal 0.
D.	$4x = 8z - 6y$	Correct.	As 6y has moved over the = sign it must become - 6y.

E. $8x + 12y = 10z.$ Incorrect.   x and y have been doubled but z has not.

Answer: E

16. If $x + 2y = 4z$. Which of the following is incorrect?

A. $2x + 4y = 8z$ B. $3x = 12z - 6y$ C. $2y - 4z = -x$
D. $2x + 2y = 4z$ E. $x + 2y - 4z = 0$

17. If $y = \frac{1}{2}x$. Which of the following is incorrect?

A. $2y = x$ B. $y/x = \frac{1}{2}$ C. $x/2 = y$
D. $y = 2x$ E. $y = x/2$

18. If $2a = b$. Which of the following is incorrect?

A. $2a/b = 1$ B. $\frac{1}{2}b = a$ C. $4a = 2b$
D. $2a - b = 0$ E. $\frac{1}{2}a = b$

19. If $x + 3y = 6z$. Which of the following is incorrect?

A. $6z - 3y = x$ B. $x + 6z = -3y$ C. $2x + 6y = 12z$
D. $x + 3y - 6z = 0$ E. $3x + 9y = 18z$

20. If $2y = x$. Which of the following is incorrect?

A. $4x = 3y$ B. $y = \frac{1}{2}x$ C. $4y = 2x$
D. $\frac{1}{2}y = x/4$ E. $2y - x = 0$

Substitution

Example

If $x = 10$ $y = 6$ $Z = 8$
$3x - 2y + z = a$
What is the value of a?

Solution:
$(3 \times 10) - (2 \times 6) + 8 =$
$30 - 12 + 8$

Answer: 26

21. If a = 10   b = 5   c = 7.

2a + 4b − c = x.   What is the value of x?

   A.   47   B.   37   C.   33   D.   30   E.   23

22. If s = 6   t = 3   u = 8.

   4s − 2t + u = r.   What is the value of r?

   A. 10   B.   14   C.   22   D.   26   E.   38

23. If e = 4   f = 9   g = 11.

   eg − f = h.   What is the value of h?

   A.   6   B.   18   C.   24   D.   35   E.   53

24. If a = 6   b = 4   c = 5.

   (a + b) − (b + c) = d.   What is the value of d?

   A.   -7   B.   -3   C.   1   D.   11   E.   19

25. If x = 5   y = 7   z = 2

   x^2 + yz = w.   What is the value of w?

   A. 19   B.   22   C.   24   D.   39   E.   42

26. If b = 2   c = 6   d = 9

   c/b + d = e.   What is the value of e?

   A. 12   B.   17   C.   21   D.   22   E.   23

27. If x = 3   y = 5   z = 8

   2x + 4z − 3y = a.   What is the value of a?

   A.   18   B.   23   C.   25   D.   33   E.   53

28. If a = 6   b = 2   c = 11

5c + 4b – 9a = d.   What is the value of d?

A.   117   B.   98   C.   52   D.   11   E.   9

29. If r = 3   s = 4   t = 5

2s – r + 2t = x.   What is the value of x ?

A.   21   B.   19   C.   17   D.   15   E.   13

30. If   a = 6   b = 4   c = 10

3c – 4a – b = d.   What is the value of d?
A. 1   B.   2   C.   3   D.   4   E.   5

Writing and using expressions to solve problems

Example

Julia is n years old. Fiona is 2 years younger than Julia. Sue is 3 times as old as Fiona. Write an expression to show Sue's age.

Solution:
Julia = n
Fiona = n – 2
Sue   = 3 (n – 2)

Answer: 3n - 6

31. Jim is 3 years younger than his brother. His brother is ¼ of his Dad's age. If Jim's age is x and his Dad's age is y, which of these is the correct expression for Jim's age?

A.   4y – 3   B.   y/4 – 3   C.   y – 3   D. y/4 + 3   E.   4 y + 3

32. Which is the same as 5 (2a – 4)?

A.   10a – 4   B.   20a – 10   C.   10a – 20   D. 10a + 20   E.   52a + 4

33. Simon is 6 years older than his sister. His sister is 1/3 of her Mum's age. If Simon's age is 'a' and his Mum's age is 'b' which of these is the correct expression for Simon's age?

A. b/3 – 6   B.   3b + 6   C.   3b – 6   D. b /3 + 6   E.   6b

34. Chloe and Daisy collect dolls. Chloe has x dolls. Daisy has 4 less than Chloe. Which expression shows the total number of dolls they have?

   A. x - 4   B.   2x – 4   C.   x + 4   D. 2x + 4   E.   4x + 2

35. George cleans cars. He uses this formula to work out how much he earns in £.

                          £12n + £20

   n = number of cars

   If he cleans 11 cars, how much does he earn?

   A. £132   B.   £141   C.   £150   D.   £152   E.   £240

36. Which is the same as 6(3b + 8)?

   A. 18b – 48   B.   18b + 48   C.   9b + 8   D.   9b + 48   E.   3b + 14

37. Three friends share a box of biscuits. Julian eats 'b' biscuits, Bob ate twice as many as Julian. Jane ate 2 less than Julian. Which expression represents the amount of biscuits eaten in total?

   A. 4b – 2   B.   2b – 2   C.   3b – 2   D. 4b + 2   E.   2b + 2

38. Jenny is x years old. Sue is 3 years older than Jenny. Rachel is 4 times as old as Sue. Which expression gives Rachel's age?

   A. 3x + 12   B.   4x + 3   C.   4x + 12   D.   4x - 12   E.   3x + 4

39. Ben has 17 pairs of socks. He has x blue pairs, 2 more black pairs than blue pairs and three times as many brown pairs as blue pairs. How many blue pairs does he have?

   A. 5   B.   3   C.   7   D.   2   E.   4

40. Fran runs y Km each weekday. She runs twice as far on Saturday and three times as far on Sunday. How many Km does she run in a week?

   A.   5y   B.   7y   C.   8y   D.   10y   E.   12y

41. Andrea's mobile phone bill, in pence, is calculated by the formula:

$$b = 800 + 9c$$

c = number of calls

If she makes 120 calls, how much is her bill?

A. £8   B.   £8.09   C.   £10.80   D.   £18.80   E.   £18.89

42. Dave and Bill collect fossils. Dave has 'a' fossils, Bill has 10 more than Dave. Which expression shows the number they have altogether?

A.   a + 10   B.   a – 10   C.   10 – 2a   D. a^2 + 10   E. 2a + 10

43. In seven years time, Jo will be x years old. How old was she 4 years ago, in terms of x?

A.   x - 11   B.   x + 11   C.   x - 4   D. x + 4   E. x + 7

44. In two years time, Mark will be x years old. How old was he five years ago, in terms of x ?

A.   x - 2   B.   x - 5   C.   x - 7   D.   7 - x   E. 5 - x

45. 4 years ago, Sue was x years old. How old is she now, in terms of x ?

A.   4x   B.   x + 4   C.   x + 2   D.   2x   E. x - 4

46. At the cinema an adult ticket costs £x and a child's ticket costs £y. How much would it cost 2 adults and 3 children, in terms of x and y ?

A.   3x + 2y   B.   5x + y   C.   2x + 3y
D.   5xy   E.   6x + 3y

47. Before a sale, Angie pays £x for a television. In the sale, it is half price. How much is it now, in terms of £x?

A.   2x   B.   x/2   C.   x - 2   D.   x + 2   E. x^2

48. A mum's age and her daughter's age total 52. The mum is 28 years older than her daughter. How old is her daughter?

A.   24   B.   18   C.   16   D.   12   E.   10

49. Archie collects toy trains. If he had 12 more trains, he would have 4 times as many as he owns. How many trains does he own?

A.   2   B.   4   C.   6   D.   8   E.   10

50. Daisy has 32 sweets. She has x milk chocolates. She has 4 more toffees than milk chocolates and twice as many dark chocolates as milk chocolates. How many milk chocolates does she have?

A.   5   B.   6   C.   7   D.   21   E.   28

Finding the nth term

Example

Find the nth term for this sequence:
2   7   12   17

Solution:

n	1	2	3	4........
pattern	2	7	12	17......

Find the difference between the numbers in the pattern.
$7 - 2 = 5$ $12 - 7 = 5$ $17 - 12 = 5$ Difference = 5

The difference (if it remains constant) is the value of n with an adjustment to equal the number in the pattern.
If n = 1   5n = 5. The first number in the pattern is 2 so subtract 3 from 5.

Answer: 5n – 3

51. Find the nth term for this sequence?

3   7   11   15

A. 4n   B.   4n – 1   C.   n – 4   D.   4n + 1   E. n – 1

52. Find the nth term for this sequence?

6   11   16   21

A. 5 – n   B.   1 – 5n   C. $5n^2$ D.   5n – 1   E.   5n + 1

53. Find the nth term for this sequence?

　　100　　94　　88　　82

A. -6n – 106　　B.　　106 – n　　C.　　6n + 6　　D.　　6n – 6　　E.　　-6n + 106

54. Find the nth term for this sequence?

　　2　　11　　20　　29

A. 9n – 7　　B.　　7n – 9　　C.　　9n – 5　　D.　　9n + 7　　E. $n^2 – 5$

55. Find the nth term for this sequence?

　　38　　35　　32　　29

A. -3n + 41　　B.　　-3n – 40　　C.　　3n + 2　　D.　　40 – 3n　　E. 3n + 3

56. Find the nth term for this sequence?

　　47　　49　　51　　53

A. n + 2　　B.　　$n^2 + 2$　　C.　　2n + 45　　D.　　n – 2　　E. 2n + 2

57. Find the nth term for this sequence?

　　4　　10　　16　　22

A.　　3n – 2　　B.　　3n – 3　　C.　　$n^2 - 2$　　D.　　6n – 3　　E. 6n - 2

58. Find the nth term for this sequence?

　　8　　11　　14　　17

A.　　3n + 3　　B.　　2n + 1　　C.　　3n + 5　　D.　　4n – 2　　E. 2n – 2

59. Find the nth term for this sequence?

　　1　　8　　15　　22

A.　　7n　　B.　　7n + 2　　C.　　7n + 6　　D.　　7n – 6　　E.　　7n – 7

60. Find the nth term for this sequence?

    5   9   13   17

  A. $4n + 1$ B. $4n + 2$ C. $4n^2$ D. $6n + 1$ E. $n^2 + 1$

Finding the mean

Example

What is the mean of: n $n - 4$ $n - 2$

Solution:

To find the mean add the terms then divide by the amount of terms.

$n + n - 4 + n - 2 = 3n - 6$
$(3n - 6) \div 3 = n - 2$

Answer: n - 2

61. What is the mean of: n $n + 2$ $n + 4$ $n + 6$

  A. $4n - 12$ B. $4n + 12$ C. $n + 2$ D. $n + 3$ E. $n + 4$

62. What is the mean of: $2n$ $3n$ $5n$ $6n$

  A. $16n$ B. $16n - 4$ C. $4n$ D. $4n - 1$ E. $4n + 1$

63. What is the mean of: $n - 8$ $n - 2$ $n - 2$ n

  A. $n - 4$ B. $n - 3$ C. $n - 2$ D. $n - 1$ E. n

64.   What is the mean of: $n + 2$ $n + 12$ $n + 1$

  A. $n + 4$ B. $n + 5$ C. $n + 6$ D. $n + 7$ E. $n + 8$

65. What is the mean of: $n - 3$ $n - 8$ $n - 4$ $n - 6$ $n - 4$

  A. $n - 7$ B. $n - 6$ C. $n - 5$ D. $n - 4$ E. $n - 3$

13. Missing number grids

Example 1

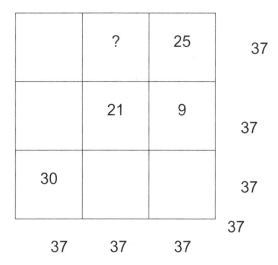

Find the missing number ?

All rows and columns total 37.
Start with a row or column which has 2 numbers eg 25 + 9 = 34
37 – 34 = 3 so bottom right square = 3
Now we can use this to find the bottom middle square.
30 + 3 = 33   37 – 33 = 4 (bottom middle)
21 + 4 = 25   37 – 25 = 12

Answer: 12

Example 2

?	32	39
18	25	32
32	39	46

Find the missing number ?
Solution:
Find the pattern inside the grid. Each row adds 7 each time so 32 – 7 =

Answer : 25

1.

	25	
18		?
	11	16

Left side: 47, 47, 47
Bottom: 47 47 47

A. 11
B. 14
C. 16
D. 18
E. 21

2.

16		
14		23
	?	17

Left side: 58
Right side: 58, 58
Bottom: 58 58 58

A. 13
B. 18
C. 21
D. 24
E. 28

3.

	?	24
	22	11
17		

Left side: 53, 53, 53
Bottom: 53 53 53

A. 9
B. 13
C. 20
D. 22
E. 23

4.

	4		
29	4		
29		5	9
29	?	12	
	29	29	29

A. 10
B. 12
C. 14
D. 15
E. 16

5.

36		12	?
36	14	8	
36			5
	36	36	36

A. 7
B. 14
C. 17
D. 19
E. 21

6.

42		13	16
42	19	?	
42	10		7
	42	42	42

A. 2
B. 9
C. 13
D. 3
E. 4

7.

	31	31	31
31	8	15	
31	?		13
31		4	

A. 3
B. 5
C. 6
D. 8
E. 12

8.

	25	25	25
25	?		
25		14	7
25		3	8

A. 4
B. 5
C. 7
D. 11
E. 14

9.

	51	51	51
51	17		32
51			?
51	16	25	

A. 2
B. 9
C. 5
D. 18
E. 10

10.

34	?	12	
34	18	14	
34			16

34   34   34

A.   6
B.   8
C.   10
D.   12
E.   14

11.

68		19	37
68		40	21
68	?		

68   68   68

A.   7
B.   12
C.   47
D.   49
E.   52

12.

49			28
49	18	?	
49	24	15	

49   49   49

A.   7
B.   10
C.   11
D.   14
E.   20

13.

4	8	16
8	16	32
16	?	64

A.   8
B.   16
C.   32
D.   36
E.   40

14.

63	52	?
52	41	30
41	30	19

A.   19
B.   31
C.   34
D.   41
E.   42

15.

17	21	25
21	25	?
25	29	33

A.   23
B.   25
C.   27
D.   29
E.   31

16.

80	72	64
72	64	56
?	56	48

A.   54
B.   58
C.   61
D.   62
E.   64

17.

?	13	20
13	20	27
20	27	34

A.   5
B.   6
C.   7
D.   9
E.   10

18.

24	12	6
12	?	3
6	3	1.5

A.   2
B.   4
C.   6
D.   8
E.   9

19.

1	3	9
?	9	27
9	27	81

A. 1
B. 3
C. 6
D. 9
E. 11

20.

1	4	16
4	16	64
16	64	?

A. 82
B. 164
C. 180
D. 256
E. 264

21.

81	89	97
97	105	?
105	113	121

A. 89
B. 97
C. 113
D. 118
E. 124

22.

32	16	?
8	4	2
4	2	1

A. 1
B. 2
C. 4
D. 8
E. 9

23.

109	100	91
100	?	82
82	73	64

A. 84
B. 86
C. 87
D. 90
E. 91

24.

73	67	61
61	55	?
55	49	43

A. 49
B. 43
C. 40
D. 73
E. 67

14. Time Problems

Time problems include 12-hour and 24-hour clock times. Be confident converting between the two. Time work also includes days, weeks and months.
Make sure you know how many days are in each of the months!

Example 1

Mr Andrews leaves home at 11:42 to drive to a meeting. The journey takes 1 hour 36 minutes. What time does he arrive at his destination? Give your answer using the 24 hour clock.

Solution:

11:42 + 1 hour = 12:42 + 36 minutes = 13:18

Answer: 13:18

Example 2

What is the combined number of days in November and August?

Solution:

November = 30 days
August   = 31 days

Answer: 61 days

1. Daisy catches the 07:23 train. The journey takes 1 hour 5 minutes. What time does she arrive at her destination?

   A.   08:08   B.   08:12   C.   08:18   D.   08:28   E.   08:32

2. A film starts at 19:20 and finishes at 21:45 How long is the film in minutes?

   A.   110   B.   125   C.   145   D.   150   E.   155

3. A cake takes 45 minutes to cook. If I put it in the oven at 15:50, what time is it ready?

   A.   16:15   B.   16:25   C.   16:35   D.   16:45   E.   16:55

4. A flight departs at 09:35 and lands at 15:25. How long is the flight?

   A.   4hr 50mins   B.   300mins   C.   5hr 30mins   D.   5hr 35mins   E.   350mins

5. Laura goes to bed at 20:10. She sleeps for 9 ½ hours. What time does she get up?

   A. 05:00   B.   05:15   C.   05.35   D.   05:40   E.   05:50

6. Tom spends 45 minutes on his maths homework and 25 minutes on his science homework. If he starts his homework at 17:20, what time does he finish?

   A. 18:30   B.   18:10   C.   18:25   D.   17:55   E.   18:40

7. The average length appointment at a Doctor's surgery is 12 minutes per patient. A Dr sees 15 patients in a morning. How long does she spend with patients that morning?

   A. 165mins   B.   180mins   C.   185mins   D.   190mins   E.   200mins

8. My watch is 11 minutes slow. It says the time is 17:51. What is the actual time?

   A. 17:40   B.   17.41   C.   18:02   D.   18:04   E.   18:05

9. I leave for school at 07:47. It takes me 21 minutes to travel there. What time do I arrive?

   A. 08:07   B.   08:08   C.   08:10   D.   08:11   E.   08:14

10. Tim took part in a sponsored silence. He started the challenge at 11.20 and ended it at 14:35. How long was he silent for?

   A. 190mins   B. 3h20mins   C. 200mins   D. 3hrs 10mins   E. 195mins

Use this train timetable to answer the following questions.

Hightown	06.12	06.49	07.36		08.45
Brentwood	06.29	07.06	07.53	08.14	0.902
Upper Norton		07.20	08.07	08.28	09.16
Sunbury	07.00	07.37	08.24	08.45	09.33
Avonmouth	07.45		09.09	09.30	10.18

11. What time does the 0736 from Hightown arrive in Sunbury?

   A. 07.37   B.   08.24   C.   08.07   D.   08.45   E.   09.09

12. How long is the journey from Upper Norton to Avonmouth?

   A. 58mins   B. 1hr   C. 1hr 2mins   D. 65mins   E. 1hr 6mins

13. Anna wants to arrive in Sunbury by 0830. What time is the latest train she can catch from Brentwood?

A. 07.06   B. 06.29   C. 06.12   D. 08.14   E. 07.36

14. Carol misses the 0612 from Hightown to Avonmouth. How long must she wait for the next train to Avonmouth?

A. 37mins   B. 57mins   C. 64mins   D. 84mins   E. 90mins

15. The 0933 from Sunbury is delayed by ¼ of an hour. What time does it arrive in Avonmouth?

A. 10.24   B. 10.29   C. 10.31   D. 10.33   E. 10.35

16. What is the total of: 52mins; 1hr 15mins; 17mins and 2hrs 43mins?

A. 303mins   B. 305mins   C. 307mins   D. 309mins   E. 311mins

17. A plane is delayed by 3hrs 40mins. It should have taken off at 14.10. The flight lasts for 2hrs 50mins. What time does it arrive?

A. 17.50   B. 19.20   C. 20.20   D. 20.40   E. 20.50

Use the following information about a race at the school sports day to answer the questions below.

	Alfie	Sam	Freddie	Oscar	Charlie
Time in sec	14.7	13.2	15.4	14.9	16.3

18. Who won the race?

A. Alfie   B. Sam   C. Freddie   D. Oscar   E. Charlie

19. What is the difference, in seconds, between Charlie's time and Sam's time?

A. 2.85   B. 2.9   C. 3.1   D. 3.2   E. 3.25

20. Who came second?

A. Alfie   B. Sam   C. Freddie   D. Oscar   E. Charlie

Use this school timetable to answer the following questions.

Lesson 1	08.45
Lesson 2	09.40
Break	10.40
Lesson 3	10.55
Lunch	12.00
Period 4	13.00
Period 5	14.10
School ends	15.20

21. How long, in minutes, is break?

A.   5   B.   10   C.   12   D.   15   E.   18

22. What is the duration of lesson 1?

A.   55mins   B.   45mins   C.   50mins   D.   40mins   E.   60mins

23. How much time is spent in lessons each day?

A. 300mins   B.   305mins   C.   310mins   D.   315mins   E.   320mins

24. A school trip leaves school at 7.50 am and returns at 3.30pm. How long are the children on the trip?

A. 450mins   B.   7hrs 40mins   C.   470mins   D.   8hrs   E.   490mins

25. How many days are there in total in June and March?

A.   58   B.   59   C.   60   D.   61   E.   61

26. How many months have 30 days?

A.   2   B.   3   C.   4   D.   5   E.   6

27. How many weeks are there in a year?

A.   50   B.   48   C.   56   D.   54   E.   52

28. If it is a leap year, how many days are there in total in January, February and March?

A.   88   B.   89   C.   90   D.   91   E.   92

29. If the 4th May is a Wednesday, what day is the 15th of May?

A. Friday   B. Saturday   C. Sunday   D. Monday   E. Tuesday

30. If the 18th April is a Monday, what day is May 3rd?

A. Monday   B. Tuesday   C. Wednesday   D. Thursday   E. Friday

15. Probability

Probability looks at the likelihood of an event occurring. It can be expressed as a fraction, decimal, percentage or in words.

Key vocabulary
Likely; unlikely; certain; impossible; even chance; greater than even; less than even.

Example

A box contains 3 blue chalks, 4 red chalks and 1 white chalk. What is the probability that I select at random,

a) a blue chalk – give your answer as a fraction
b) a red chalk – give your answer as a decimal
c) a white chalk – give your answer as a percentage
d) a green chalk – give your answer in words
e) a blue or red chalk – give your answer as a fraction

Solution

Add together all the chalks.
3+4+1=8
a) There are 3 blue chalks out of a total of 8 chalks.
Answer : 3/8

b) There are 4 red chalks out of 8 chalks which is equal to ½. Convert to a decimal.
Answer : 0.5

c) There is 1 white chalk out of 8 chalks which is equal to 1/8. Convert to a percentage.
Answer : 12.5%

d) There are no green chalks.
Answer : impossible

e) Add the blue and red chalks together. 3+4=7 out of 8 chalk in total.
Answer : 7/8

1. A bag contains 4 red balls, 6 blue balls, 3 yellow balls and 2 green balls. What is the probability that I select at random:

a) A red ball?

   A.   2/15   B.   3/15   C. 4/15   D.   6/15   E.   10/15

b) A yellow or green ball?

    A.   1/3   B.   1/5   C.   1/15   D.   2/15   E.   2/3

c) An orange ball?

    A.   1/15   B.   2/15   C.   1/3   D.   3/15   E.   0

2. There are 30 chocolates in a box. 12 are milk chocolate, 10 dark chocolate and the rest are toffees. If I choose a sweet at random, what is the probability that it will be -

a) A milk chocolate?

    A.   1/5   B.   2/5   C.   3/5   D.   7/15   E.   8/15

b) A toffee?

    A.   6/15   B.   7/30   C.   ¼   D.   4/15   E.   1/3

3. A spinner is divided into 8 sections. Each section contains a number. These are: 1, 4, 3, 3, 2, 1, 4, 3. What is the probability that when the spinner is spun it lands on an odd number?

    A.   3/8   B.   ½   C.   5/8   D.   ¾   E.   7/8

4. I roll a standard dice. What is the probability that it will land on a prime number?

    A.   1/6   B.   1/3   C.   5/6   D.   2/3   E.   ½

5. A bag contains 5 blue marbles, 10 green marbles, 3 red marbles and 2 white marbles. In which of the answers below are both statements correct?

    A.   You are certain to pick a marble.
          You have a greater than even chance of picking a blue marble.

    B.   You have an even chance of selecting a green marble.
          You have a greater than even chance of selecting a white marble.

    C.   You have a less than even chance of selecting a red marble.
          You have an even chance of picking a blue marble.

    D.   You have an even chance of selecting a green marble.
          You have a less than even chance of selecting a red marble.

    E.   You are certain to pick a marble.
          You have an even chance of selecting a red marble.

6. The probability of it snowing in March is 0.09. What is the probability that it does not snow?

    A. 0.01   B. 0.19   C. 0.81   D. 0.9   E. 0.91

7. In a box of 24 biscuits, 8 are ginger biscuits, 6 are shortbreads and the rest are chocolate biscuits. What is the probability that I select at random -

a) A shortbread?

    A. 1/3   B. ¼   C. 1/5   D. 1/6   E. 1/8

b) A chocolate biscuit?

    A. 7/12   B. 8/24   C. 5/12   D. 7/24   E. 5/8

c) Either a chocolate or a ginger biscuit?

    A. 2/3   B. ¾   C. 5/6   D. 10/12   E. 1/3

8. I have 12 tins in my cupboard. 4 contain fruit, 6 contain soup and 2 are beans. What is the probability that I select at random a tin of fruit?

    A. 1/6   B. ½   C. ¼   D. 1/3   E. 1/12

9. In a bowl of fruit there are 4 apples, 6 bananas and 2 peaches. What is the probability that I select at random a peach?

    A. Less than even   B. Even   C. Greater than even
    D. Impossible   E. Certain

10. A spinner is divided into 10 sections. 1 is green, 3 are blue, 5 are red and 1 is yellow. When the spinner is spun what it is the probability that it lands on a red section?

    A. Less than even   B. Even   C. Greater than even
    D. Impossible   E. Certain

11. A lucky dip contains the following prizes: 12 boxes of chocolates, 5 bottles of wine and 3 candles. What is the probability that I select at random -

a) a box of chocolates?

    A. Less than even   B. Even   C. Greater than even
    D. Impossible   E. Certain

b) a teddy bear?

A. Less than even   B. Even   C. Greater than even
D. Impossible   E. Certain

c) a bottle of wine?

A. Less than even   B. Even   C. Greater than even
D. Impossible   E. Certain

12. The probability that it will rain tomorrow is 0.57. What is the probability that it will not rain?

A. 0.33   B. 0.43   C. 0.45   D. 0.53   E. 0.54

13. A tool-box contains the following items: 4 screwdrivers, 2 chisels, 1 tape measure, and 1 saw. In which of the answers below are both statements correct?

A. You are certain to pick a tool.
You have a greater than even chance of picking a screwdriver.

B. You have a less than even chance of picking a screwdriver.
You have a less than even chance of picking a chisel.

C. You have an even chance of picking a screwdriver.
You have a less than even chance of picking a tape measure.

D. You have a greater than even chance of picking a chisel.
You have a less than even chance of picking a saw.

E. You are certain to pick a screwdriver.
You have a greater than even chance of picking a saw.

14. In a class of 25 children, 13 are boys and the rest are girls. Assuming all the children are present, what is the probability that in a raffle a girl's name will be randomly selected?

A. 12%   B. 24%   C. 38%   D. 48%   E. 52%

15. A road has 30 houses of which 18 are detached and the rest are semi- detached. All the house numbers are put into a competition to win a makeover. What is the probability that a semi-detached house is chosen at random?

A. 30%   B. 40%   C. 50%   D. 60%   E. 70%

16. A box contains scarves and hats. If there are 21 hats and 9 scarves, what is the probability that I select at random, a hat?

   A.   0.2   B.   0.3   C.   0.7   D.   0.8   E.   0.9

17. A teacher has 40 books to mark. 16 are Maths books, 10 English books and the remainder are Science books. If she randomly selects a book, what is the probability that she selects -

a) A Science book?

   A.   15%   B.   20%   C.   25%   D.   30%   E.   35%

b) An English book?

   A.   0.15   B.   0.2   C.   0.25   D.   0.3   E.   0.35

c) A Maths book?

   A.   2/5   B.   9/20   C.   ½   D.   11/20   E.   3/5

d) A Maths or English book?

   A.   0.55   B.   0.45   C.   0.85   D.   0.75   E.   0.65

18. A box of smarties has 8 blue ones, 6 orange ones, 9 yellow ones, 4 red ones and 5 brown ones. What is the probability that I randomly select -

a) a blue or orange one?

   A.   13/32   B.   7/16   C.   3/8   D.   15/32   E.   9/16

b) A red one?

   A.   8%   B.   9.5%   C.   10.5%   D.   12.5%   E.   14%

c) A yellow, red or brown one?

   A.   7/16   B.   9/16   C.   11/16   D.   5/8   E.   7/8

19. The probability of a football team scoring a goal is 0.68. What is the probability that they do not score?

   A.   0.12   B.   0.22   C.   0.32   D.   0.42   E.   0.52

20. A pencil-case contains 2 rubbers, 8 coloured pencils, 2 pencil sharpeners, 4 lead pencils, 3 pens and a ruler. What is the probability that I randomly select

a) A pencil?

    A.   0.6   B.   0.48   C.   0.12   D.   0.7   E.   0.62

b) A pencil sharpener?

    A.   2%   B.   4%   C.   8%   D.   10%   E.   12%

c) A ruler?

    A.   1%   B.   2%   C.   3%   D.   4%   E.   5%

d) A pen?

    A.   less than even chance   B.   even chance   C.   impossible
    D.   greater than even chance   E.   certain

16. Multiplication and Division Problems

Example 1

A farmer stores bales of hay in stacks of 18. If he has 47 stacks, how many bales does he have?

Solution

Multiply 47 x 18

```
          47
     x    18
         376
         470
Answer :  846
```

Example 2

How many books are left over if 240 books are packed into boxes of 25?

Solution

Divide 240 by 25. The remainder is the answer.

```
        009 r 15
   25 / 240
```

Answer : 15

1. A gardener plants 18 rows of beans. There are 17 plants per row. How many beans are planted?

   A.   270   B.   286   C.   306   D.   316   E.   326

2. 1679 lightbulbs are produced in a factory. They are packed into 23 crates. How many are there per crate?

   A.   69   B.   71   C.   72   D.   73   E.   75

3. £32,500 is won in the lottery. It is shared equally between 13 people. How much does each person receive?

   A.   £2000   B.   £2250   C.   £2500   D.   £2750   E.   £2950

4. Andy saves £19 a month for 2 years. How much has he saved?

   A.   £456   B.   £452   C.   £446   D.   £486   D.   £466

5. An examiner marks 45 papers per hour. If she works 6 hours a day for 8 days, how many papers does she mark?

   A.   1860   B.   1960   C.   2060   D.   2160   E.   2260

6. How many biscuits are left over if 470 biscuits are put into packs of 26?

   A.   1   B.   2   C.   4   D.   5   E.   9

7. A box of pencils costs £1.49, a box of pens costs £2.85. Freddie buys 3 boxes of pencils and 2 boxes of pens. How much does he spend in total?

   A.   £10.17   B.   £7.32   C.   £7.19   D.   £8.68   E.   £13.02

8. A greengrocer has 16 boxes of oranges. Each box contains 54 oranges. How many oranges does he have?

   A.   824   B.   834   C.   844   D.   854   E.   864

9. Amanda earns £29,400 per year. How much does she earn each month?

   A.   £2135   B.   £2245   C.   £2360   D.   £2420   E.   £2450

10. A school goes on a camping trip with 94 children. Each tent sleeps 6 people. How many tents are needed to sleep all the people?

    A.   14   B.   15   C.   16   D.   17   E.   18

11. Ian collects stamps. His album has 64 pages, on each page he has 25 stamps. How many stamps does he have in total?

    A.   1600   B.   1610   C.   1620   D.   1630   E.   1640

12. How many apples are left over if 1486 apples are packed in boxes of 65?

    A.   44   B.   47   C.   49   D.   53   E.   56

13. A box of chocolates contains 32 chocolates. How many chocolates are there in 26 boxes?

  A.   800   B.   832   C.   858   D.   862   E.   888

14. £381 is shared equally between 4 people. How much does each person receive?

  A.   £94.25   B.   £94.75   C.   £95.25   D.   £95.50   E.   £95.75

15. Eggs are packed in boxes of a dozen. How many full boxes can be made from 220 eggs?

  A.   15   B.   16   C.   17   D.   18   E.   19

16. A bookshelf has 14 shelves. Each shelf contains 36 books. How many books are there, in total?

  A.   498   B.   501   C.   504   D.   506   E.   510

17. Chris spends £31.50 on 75 plants at the local nursery. If all plants are priced equally, how much does she pay, per plant?

  A.   29p   B.   35p   C.   39p   D.   42p   E.   43p

18. A cake weighs 1.5Kg. It is cut equally into 8 pieces. How much does each slice weigh?

  A.   167.5g   B.   157.5g   C.   177.5g   D.   187.5g   E.   197.5g

19. There are 26 rows of chairs in a hall. Each row has 28 chairs in it. How many chairs are there?

  A.   700   B.   728   C.   746   D.   784   E.   798

20. If a farmer plants 254 rows of cabbages, with 64 plants in a row, how many cabbages has he planted?

  A.   15,748   B.   16,002   C.   16,064   D.   16,146   E.   16,256

21. If 247 x 32 = 7904, what is 16 x 247?

  A.   988   B.   1976   C.   2463   D.   3952   E.   5904

22. If 186 x 14 = 2604, what is 186 x 28?

  A.   5208   B.   5604   C.   4602   D.   1302   E.   3204

23. If 37 x 24 = 888, what is 3.7 x 2.4?

  A.   0.088   B.   0.88   C.   808   D.   88.8   E.   8.88

24. If 4.9 x 12 = 58.8, what is 49 x 12?

    A.   0.588   B.   5.88   C.   588   D.   5088   E.   5880

25. If 8.5 x 7.2 = 61.2, what is 85 x 72?

    A.   0.612   B.   6.12   C.   612   D.   6120   E.   61200

26. Calculate 721 ÷ 4

    A.   170.25   B.   180.25   C.   180.5   D.   180.75   E.   181.2

27. Calculate 361 ÷ 8

    A.   450.125   B. 45.125   C.   45.14   D.   46.12   E.   46.125

28. Calculate 542 ÷ 8

    A.   67.75   B.   68.25   C.   68.75   D.   69.25   E.   69.58

29. Calculate 824 ÷ 5

    A.   264.5   B.   263.8   C.   164.8   D.   163.8   E.   162.5

30. Calculate 321 ÷ 6

    A.   33.56   B.   43.5   C.   53.25   D.   53.5   E.   54.5

17. Fraction Work

This section covers several fraction related topics that may be tested in the 11+.
It includes work on equivalent fractions, stating one amount as a fraction of another, calculating fractions, decimals and percentages, deciding which answer has a different value and identifying the largest fraction, decimal or percentage in a list.

Equivalent Fractions

Example

Which of these fractions is not equivalent to 5/7 ?

A. 35/49   B. 15/21   C. 45/63   D. 10/14   E. 30/35

Solution

A. 5/7 = 35/49   (numerator and denominator multiplied by 7)
B. 5/7 = 15/21   (numerator and denominator multiplied by 3)
C. 5/7 = 45/63   (numerator and denominator multiplied by 9)
D. 5/7 = 10/14   (numerator and denominator multiplied b 2)
E. 5/7 DOES NOT = 30/35   (the numerator has been multiplied by 6 but not the denominator)

Answer : 30/35 = E

1. Which of these fractions is not equivalent to 3/5?

    A.   9/15   B.   12/20   C.   27/45   D.   25/40   E.   6/10

2. Which of these fractions is not equivalent to 2/3?

    A.   6/9   B.   10/18   C.   20/30   D.   18/27   E.   24/36

3. Which of these fractions is not equivalent to ¾?

    A.   45/60   B.   100/120   C.   60/80   D.   36/48   E.   30/40

4. Which of these fractions is equivalent to 5/6?

    A.   21/30   B.   65/72   C.   35/42   D.   32/36   E.   48/60

5. Which of these fractions is equivalent to 7/8?

    A.   26/32   B.   21/25   C.   63/82   D.   55/64   E.   42/48

6. Which of these fractions is equivalent to 9/11?

   A.   36/44   B.   54/60   C.   18/24   D.   70/88   E.   98/121

Which has the largest value?

Example

Which of these is the largest?

A. 14/20   B. 0.14   C.   14/25   D. 24%   E. 68%

Solution

Convert all into decimals then compare.
A = 0.70   B = 0.14   C = 0.56   D = 0.24   E = 0.68

Answer : A

7. Which of these is the largest?

   A.   12/20   B.   7/10   C.   0.9   D.   72%   E.   4/5

8. Which of these is the largest?

   A.   14%   B.   0.04   C.   6/50   D.   1/8   E.   0.12

9. Which of these is the largest?

   A. 0.69   B.   17/25   C.   67%   D.   35/50   E.   0.68

10. Which of these is the largest?

   A.   4/5   B.   0.77   C.   6/8   D.   79%   E.   7/10

Which has a different answer?

Example

Which of these has a different answer to the others?

- A. 20% of 185
- B. 0.1 of 370
- C. ¼ of 148
- D. 5% of 740
- E. 0.75 of 48

Solution

Calculate each answer. Compare answers.

A = 37
B = 37
C = 37
D = 37
E = 36

Answer : E

11. Which of these has a different answer to the others?

- A. 2/5 of 85
- B. 50% of 68
- C. 0.4 of 85
- D. 10% of 340
- E. 60% of 90

12. Which of these has a different answer to the others?

- A. 0.06 of 30
- B. 3/50 of 30
- C. 6% of 30
- D. 0.6 of 30
- E. 6/100 of 30

13. Which of these has a different answer to the others?

- A. 80% of 100
- B. ¼ of 320
- C. 0.1 of 800
- D. 20% of 400
- E. 70% of 90

14. Which of these has a different answer to the others?

- A. 4/8 of 180
- B. 0.5 of 180
- C. 0.05 of 180
- D. 50/100 of 180
- E. 50% of 180

15. Which of these has a different answer to the others?

- A. ¼ of 80
- B. 0.2 of 80
- C. 25% of 80
- D. 2/8 of 80
- E. 0.25 of 80

16. Which of these has a different answer to the others?

    A.   40% of 80   B.   10% of 300   C.   0.3 of 100   D. ½ of 60
    E.   0.25 of 120

17. Which of these has a different answer to the others?

    A.   0.2 of 40   B.   1/5 of 40   C.   0.5 of 40   D.   4/20 of 40
    E.   20% of 40

18.   Which of these has a different answer to the others?

    A.   0.5 of 4   B.   50% of 2   C.   5% of 20   D.   0.05 of 20
    E.   10% of 10

19. Which of these has a different answer to the others?

    A.   20% of 60   B.   ½ of 24   C.   0.25 of 48   D.   25% of 40
    E.   1/3 of 36

20.   Which of these has a different answer to the others?

    A.   0.08 of 100   B.   4/50 of 100   C.   8/100 of 100   D. 8% of 100
    E.   4% of 100

Stating one amount as a fraction of another

Example

What fraction of 7 litres is 550ml?

Solution

First convert to the same unit of measurement. Write as a fraction. Simplify.

7 L = 7000ml
550/7000 = 11/140

Answer : 11/140

21. What fraction of 3 Kg is 800g?

    A.   3/8   B.   8/10   C.   8/12   D.   4/15   E.   11/20

22. What fraction of 5 Km is 2.8Km?

   A. 2/5   B. 3/5   C. 3/25   D. 8/25   E. 14/25

23. What fraction of 2 L is 900ml?

   A. ½   B. 2/5   C. 9/10   D. 9/20   E. 9/40

24. What fraction of 3 hours is 1 hour 20 minutes?

   A. 1/3   B. 2/3   C. 4/9   D. 5/9   E. 10/12

25. What fraction of 1 week is 2 days?

   A. 1/7   B. 2/7   C. 1/3   D. 2/3   E. 2/5

26. What fraction of 6Km is 4.5Km?

   A. 1/3   B. 2/3   C. ¼   D. ¾   E. 5/6

27. What fraction of 2 Kg is 600g?

   A. 3/10   B. 2/3   C. 3/5   D. 2/6   E. 6/10

28. What fraction of 1 year is 8 months?

   A. 1/8   B. 1/3   C. 2/3   D. 3/12   E. 4/12

29. What fraction of 1cm is 4mm?

   A. ¼   B. 2/5   C. 1/10   D. ¾   E. 2/10

30. What fraction of 4m is 0.3m?

   A. ¼   B. ¾   C. 3/40   D. 1/40   E. 4/100

ANSWERS

Unit 1 – Fractions of whole numbers

1. C	2. A	3. D	4. B	5. E	6. D	7. B	8. A	9. D	10. D
11. A	12. B	13. E	14. C	15. C	16. C	17. A	18. B	19. B	20. A
21. D	22. B	23. C	24. B	25. D	26. B	27. E	28. D	29. E	30. C

Unit 2 – Simplifying Fractions

1. C	2. B	3. D	4. E	5. A	6. B	7. A	8. C	9. B	10. D
11. D	12. B	13. C	14. A	15. D	16. B	17. C	18. B	19. D	20. E
21. B	22. E	23. A	24. C	25. D	26. A	27. E	28. B	29. C	30. D

Unit 3 – Converting Fractions into Percentages

1. C	2. B	3. A	4. D	5. B	6. D	7. C	8. D	9. E	10. A
11. B	12. C	13. D	14. C	15. E	16. C	17. E	18. D	19. B	20. B
21. A	22. A	23. B	24. B	25. C	26. E	27. C	28. A	29. B	30. D

Unit 4 – Finding Percentages of Amounts

1. E	2. A	3. D	4. E	5. B	6. A	7. D	8. B	9. C	10. D
11. E	12. B	13. E	14. A	15. B	16. D	17. B	18. C	19. E	20. A
21. D	22. A	23. E	24. B	25. C	26. B	27. C	28. C	29. D	30. D

Unit 5 – Volume, Area and Perimeter

1. E	2. E	3. C	4. D	5. A	6. B	7. C	8. A	9. C	10. A
11. C	12. E	13. D	14. B	15. A	16. B	17. D	18. C	19. E	20. D
21. D	22. C	23. B	24. D	25. E	26. B	27. A	28. C	29. B	30. E

Unit 6 – Ratio

1. D	2. A	3. B	4. B	5. D	6. E	7. B	8. C	9. B	10. D
11. A	12. D	13. A	14. C	15. E	16. D	17. C	18. A	19. B	20. E
21. E	22. B	23. D	24. A	25. E	26. A	27. A	28. D	29. C	30. C
31. E	32. B	33. C	34. D	35. B	36. E	37. C	38. C	39. B	40. A

Unit 7 – Measurement – Metric and Imperial

1. B	2. E	3. D	4. C	5. D	6. D	7. E	8. D	9. D	10. D
11. C	12. A	13. C	14. D	15. E	16. C	17. B	18. C	19. C	20. E
21. B	22. D	23. A	24. A	25. C	26. C	27. E	28. B	29. C	30. D

Unit 8 – Averages

1a. C	1b. A	2a. B	2b. B	3. C	4a. C	4b. A	4c. D	4d. B	5a. D
5b. A	5c. C	6a. B	6b. C	6c. A	7. B	8. E	9. E	10. A	11a. C
11b. E	12. A	13. E	14a. D	14b. D	15. C	16a. A	16b. D	16c. D	16d. E
16e. B	16f. E	17a. C	17b. D	17c. C	18a. D	18b. C	18c. A	19a. D	19b. C
19c. B	19d. C	20a. D	20b. C	20c. C					

Unit 9 – 2D and 3D Shapes and Angles

1. B	2. E	3. B	4. C	5. D	6. C	7. B	8. C	9. D	10. A
11. A	12. C	13. D	14. C	15. E	16. C	17. B	18. A	19. B	20. D
21. B	22. D	23. A	24. D	25. E	26. E	27. D	28. B	29. B	30. C

Unit 10- General Number Questions

1. B	2. C	3. B	4. A	5. C	6. A	7. C	8. E	9. D	10. E
11. B	12. C	13. E	14. B	15. C	16. D	17. D	18. A	19. A	20. C
21. C	22. C	23. E	24. D	25. B	26. A	27. E	28. E	29. C	30. D

Unit 11 – Scale

1. B	2. E	3. A	4. D	5. E	6. C	7. D	8. A	9. D	10. C
11. C	12. D	13. E	14. A	15. C	16. D	17. D	18. B	19. B	20. A
21. C	22. D	23. E	24. D	25. D	26. C	27. B	28. E	29. C	30. A

Unit 12 - Algebra

1. C	2. B	3. A	4. D	5. E	6. B	7. C	8. D	9. A	10. C
11. E	12. A	13. C	14. D	15. E	16. D	17. D	18. E	19. B	20. A
21. C	22. D	23. D	24. C	25. D	26. A	27. B	28. E	29. D	30. B
31. B	32. C	33. D	34. B	35. D	36. B	37. A	38. C	39. B	40. D
41. D	42. E	43. A	44. C	45. B	46. C	47. B	48. D	49. B	50. C
51. B	52. E	53. E	54. A	55. A	56. C	57. E	58. C	59. D	60. A
61. D	62. C	63. B	64. B	65. C					

Unit 13 – Missing Number Grids

1. D	2. A	3. B	4. A	5. C	6. E	7. C	8. C	9. B	10. A
11. D	12. E	13. C	14. D	15. D	16. E	17. B	18. C	19. B	20. D
21. C	22. D	23. E	24. A						

Unit 14 – Time Problems

1. D	2. C	3. C	4. E	5. D	6. A	7. B	8. C	9. B	10. E
11. B	12. C	13. A	14. D	15. D	16. C	17. D	18. B	19. C	20. A
21. D	22. A	23. E	24. B	25. D	26. C	27. E	28. D	29. C	30. B

Unit 15 – Probability

1a. C	1b. A	1c. E	2a. B	2b. D	3. C	4. E	5. D	6. E	7a. B
7b. C	7c. B	8. D	9. A	10. B	11a. C	11b. D	11c. A	12. B	13. C
14. D	15. B	16. C	17a. E	17b. C	17c. A	17d. E	18a. B	18b. D	18c. B
19. C	20a. A	20b. D	20c. E	20d. A					

Unit 16 – Multiplication and Division Problems

1. C	2. D	3. C	4. A	5. D	6. B	7. A	8. E	9. E	10. C
11. A	12. E	13. B	14. C	15. D	16. C	17. D	18. D	19. B	20. E
21. D	22. A	23. E	24. C	25. D	26. B	27. B	28. A	29. C	30. D

Unit 17 – Fraction Work

1. D	2. B	3. B	4. C	5. E	6. A	7. C	8. A	9. D	10. A
11. E	12. D	13. E	14. C	15. B	16. A	17. C	18. A	19. D	20. E
21. D	22. E	23. D	24. C	25. B	26. D	27. A	28. C	29. B	30. C

Printed in Great Britain
by Amazon